*"An instant classic, the seasons change, but the lessons are timeless and gifts to those when they are needed most. This book eases the journey and accelerates the transition process."*

> —**David Kasiarz**, Senior Vice President, Global Total Rewards and Learning
> The American Express Company

*"I loved your book and have read parts two or three times. As a Next Season graduate soon to be three times, I reflected on things I did well and things I wish I had done differently. The biggest learning for me as I enter my Next Season is to take time to really think about how I wish and intend to spend my time. I've made a commitment to take zero offers for three months. After being a corporate executive for over 20 years and two CEO jobs at big non-profits, it's time to rest, reflect, renew, and rethink. You've provided a perfect guide to keep Type A personalities focused on staying busy but in different and potentially more meaningful ways."*

> —**Vicki Escarra**, Global CEO
> Opportunity International
>
> Former CEO, Feeding America
>
> Former EVP, Chief Marketing Officer, Delta Air Lines, Inc.

*"The insights and help shared by Dr. Leslie Braksick are priceless. She has fog lights that allow her to help someone approaching retirement see the future clearly and plan for what can be the best chapter in one's life. I have seen her do this live with top companies, and she has now translated this experience into* Your Next Season *in a powerful and thoughtful way."*

> —**Edward A. Kangas**, Former Global Chairman and Chief Executive Officer
> Deloitte Touche Tohmatsu Limited
>
> Chairman, Board of Directors, Deutsche Bank USA Corporation
>
> Lead Director, Board of Directors, United Technologies Corporation
>
> Chair, Governance Committee, Board of Directors,
> Tenet Healthcare Corporation
>
> Chair, Audit Committee, Board of Directors, Intelsat S.A.
>
> Chair, Audit Committee, Board of Directors, Hovanian Enterprises, Inc.

*"Like so many retiring university presidents, I was not only leaving the position that had been my life for more than a decade, but moving out of the president's home and relocating to a new city.* Your Next Season *delivered the practical tools, inspiration, and advice that I needed to start a personally fulfilling and intellectually stimulating next chapter!"*

> —**Anne Steele**, Retired, President
> Muskingum University

I

*"Everyone will have a Next Season in life. The difference between those of us who survive it versus thrive in it will be the purposeful thinking, honesty about ourselves, and decisive actions we bring to the process. This book gives us all a roadmap, a 'how-to' guide with insights from others who have designed their paths with intention. It is a can't-miss read for anyone who wants to live the next chapter of life fully and with impact."*

–**Brenda Wensil**, Chief Customer Experience Officer
U.S. Department of Education, Office of Federal Student Aid

*"You captured my exact feelings during my transition! I recommend* Your Next Season *to anyone beginning this journey. Pace yourself as you decide how to finish well."*

–**Joe Price**, Retired, President of Consumer and Small Business Banking
Bank of America

Chair, Board of Directors, Habitat for Humanity International

*"Whether suddenly or with time to plan, Drs. Braksick and Innes provide invaluable advice and tools to effectively deal with the critical first transition step, "Pause," or discernment before leaping ahead. The transition of 'seasons' for an executive is one of the most important and scariest lifetime events, but with Drs. Braksick and Innes' advice and tools, successful navigation is made much easier."*

–**Jim Unruh**, Founding Principal
Alerion Capital Group, LLC

*"Packed with the experiences of others, this is a thoughtful piece on transitioning from a highly active career into the Next Season in life. A worthwhile read for those interested in successfully making the journey."*

–**Ed Galante**, Retired, Senior Vice President
ExxonMobil Corporation
Corporate Director

*"Have you ever thought how an astronaut slows down from flying at 15,000 miles per hour to a soft landing without burning up on reentry? Full of interesting experiences and distilled into usable 'pearls of wisdom,' this very readable and entertaining book by Drs. Braksick and Innes is the manual for the highly successful to slow down to the speed of life and their happy reentry into their retirement."*

–**Rob Cañizares**, Retired, President
MSA International

*"Drs. Braksick and Innes have created a well-researched and accessible guide for executives transitioning away from the structured momentum of corporate life. They provide building blocks for retired executives and their spouses to help explore and optimize a new world of choice, opportunity, and purpose in the seasons ahead."*

**– Alan Kelly**, Retired, President
ExxonMobil Downstream Marketing

Adjunct Professor, Wake Forest University

*"Essential reading for executives and their spouses transitioning from corporate life to a future of unbounded possibilities."*

**– Carol Kelly**, Executive Spouse

*"If you're an executive close to retirement, your world is about to be rocked in a multitude of ways. Through stories and tips shared by recently retired executives, this book will help you 'see the change, so you can be the change,' to successfully lead yourself, your family, and your company into Your Next Season of significance."*

**– Julie Smith**, Ph.D., Chief Executive Officer
ChangePartner

*"Navigating the transition with the support and friendship of Leslie helped me so much. It is guidance I sought and benefited from greatly. I am glad I did not try and go it alone. Her experience with so many details of a transition like mine remains invaluable as I progress to my Next Season."*

**– John W. Thiel**, Former Head
Merrill Lynch Wealth Management

*"Clear. Courageous. And with unvarnished advice, this book is practical from beginning to end. A must-read for executives considering their next phase and the companies that employ them. Fast-paced and replete with compelling anecdotes and personal examples, the book concludes on a high by offering worksheets and prompts that the reader can benefit from immediately. Buy your copy today!"*

**– Mindy Mackenzie**, CEO Advisor and WSJ bestselling author of
*The Courage Solution - The Power of Truth Telling With Your Boss, Peers, and Team*
MM Enterprises

*"Your Next Season thankfully disrupts the notion of retirement as a form of surrender. The authors provide a simple call to action that resets boundaries for relevancy and gives permission for continued contributions to things that matter."*

**– Robb Webb**, Chief Human Resources Officer
Tenet Healthcare Corporation

*"An excellent guide for executives transitioning into retirement. While the authors have used their extensive experience and interviews to focus on 'senior' executives, I believe this book is an appropriate guide for many non-executives approaching retirement."*

> **–Michael Ramage**, Retired, Executive Vice President
> ExxonMobil Research and Engineering Company

*"To the best of my knowledge, this book is a first. It thoroughly addresses the important subject of how to make your transition from a life of running hard every day to one of using your gifts and experience in a way that is purposeful and fulfilling. It explains the process, provides real-life examples, and includes tools to guide you and your spouse/partner on the journey."*

> **–Frank Berardi**, Retired, Director of Employee Development
> The Allstate Corporation

*"A great guide for the retiring executive, this book provides a wonderful path though the transition from retirement to a Next Season. It explores the thoughts and feelings that often accompany retirement and the uncertainty beyond. It is well-written, complete with great advice, thoughts from many executives that have blazed the trail already, and practical tips on how to plan and execute the process."*

> **–Richard Downen**, Retired, Executive
> Bank of America

*"Business executives have led organization change most of their lives, yet we have not prepared these important people to effectively manage their own life transitions. This field guide has practical advice and tools for retiring executives, or for anyone contemplating a major career change. A must-read for all corporate Baby Boomers!"*

> **–Dan Hawkins**, President
> Summit Leadership Partners LLC
>
> Former Fortune 500 Executive

*"Reading* Your Next Season *will help senior executives replace fear of retirement with joyful anticipation of the future. Practical tools and engaging testimonials encourage executives to reflect, dream, and envision a successful Next Season. This book is a must-read for leaders nearing retirement!"*

> **–Nancy Bunce**, Partner
> Morningstar Song LLC

*"Good read and so true. Recommend it to anyone seeking to make a shift as it really captures the changes you will face."*

> **–Ronald A. Rittenmeyer**, Retired, Chairman, President, and
> Chief Executive Officer
> Electronic Data Systems

*"What a wonderful collection of sage advice for executives transitioning from warp-speed lifestyles and slammed calendars to more peaceful lives grounded in greater purpose. Drs. Braksick and Innes give us a compelling reminder that it's OK to press the 'pause' button and take some time to plan for a Next Season not orchestrated by the world around us, but rather shaped by our own gifts, aspirations, and imaginations . . . and, of course, a few whispers from above."*

    **– Mike Sharp**, Retired, Corporate Real Estate Executive
    Bank of America

    Founder & Owner Lighthouse Consulting Corporation

*"Retirement from intense business careers is an abrupt affair. Your Next Season provides more than enough for new retirees to work with from a large cross-section of people who have already been there. Active engagement in the future is the way forward. To succeed, you need something of equal imaginative power to match what your career gave you."*

    **– W.A. Macdonald**, President
    W.A. Macdonald Associates, Inc.

*"Your Next Season skillfully takes readers from a life in the 'frying pan' of corporate life to a life built on purpose and personal fulfillment. Leslie Braksick and Bill Innes have crafted a smart, entertaining, and actionable blueprint for anyone planning the Next Season of their life."*

    **– Gary Sheffer**, Retired, VP of Communications and Public Affairs
    General Electric Company

*"Bill Innes and Leslie Braksick have written a book that should be read by all executives. All executives will face the decisions that Innes and Braksick discuss in* Your Next Season. *Unfortunately, many executives put off these decisions—and the requisite planning that goes into them—far too long. Multiple personal examples from real life executives will make it clear that using the principles and actions described in* Your Next Season *will help enhance an executive's next position and/or retirement."*

    **– Wood Parker**, Chairman, Leadership Development Council
    Global Good Fund

*"Retirement looks different today, and the insights here help spark new ideas and offer practical advice and fresh perspectives. The thoughtful analysis and real-life examples are extremely beneficial for those planning their Next Season."*

    **– Andrea Smith**, Chief Administrative Officer
    Bank of America

"'Yoda' is the word that aptly implies the wisdom contained in Drs. Braksick and Innes' Your Next Season: Advice for Executives on Transitioning from Intense Careers to Fulfilling Next Seasons. If you are headed toward a change of seasons, do yourself a huge favor—read this book, and act on it! Not only will you have the wisdom of Yoda from the two authors who are fonts of wisdom, but you will benefit from the dozens of lessons shared from clients just like you who they have counseled over the decades. This is by far the best inspirational and practical guide I have read on this topic. Applying the lessons shared herein will change your life!"

– **David Simms**, President
Olive Tree Impact Foundation

Former Executive Chairman and President, Opportunity International

"Start planning for life after your hectic career before you leave. There is no one right answer and, clearly, no silver bullet on how to transition. As they say, 'to each his own.' This advice, however, does give a list of the many things one needs to consider when approaching the 'departure' date, whatever the reason. The range of advice is broad and, importantly, real-life examples help to illustrate best practices that one may choose to adopt. As I look back, I wish I had this to read a year or two before I retired. I may—no, I would—have done some things differently. No reason to make the same mistakes I did. This advice will help amplify and underscore the words a transition counselor will provide . . . the two go hand and hand. As an aside, after almost two years into my Next Season, it was great to read this sage advice and fine tune accordingly."

– **Neil Cotty**, Retired, Chief Accounting Officer
Bank of America

"After 20 years of teaching and coaching successful leaders on a journey 'From Success to Significance,' I believe that Your Next Season is packed full of practical wisdom and expertise that will help you avoid costly, but common, mistakes at retirement. Your most creative and productive years could be ahead."

– **Lloyd Reeb**, Primary Spokesperson
Halftime Institute

"Senior executives thrive when they have the opportunity to build and execute plans that drive value for their key stakeholders. Your Next Season provides these executives with a thoughtful and holistic plan to put themselves in the stakeholder seat. That journey is expertly guided by the experience and insights of Drs. Braksick and Innes. This is a great read for executives as well as the HR professionals that support them."

– **Marty Gervasi**, Chief Human Resources Officer
The Hartford Financial Services Group, Inc.

# Your Next Season

Advice for Executives on Transitioning from Intense Careers to Fulfilling Next Seasons

**Leslie W. Braksick**, Ph.D. • **William R. K. Innes**, D.Eng.

For permission to use any portion of this book, please email info@mynextseason.com or contact My Next Season, 6201 Fairview Road, Suite 200, Charlotte, NC 28210.

Library of Congress Cataloging-in-Publication Data

Braksick, Leslie W.

Innes, William R. K.

*Your Next Season: Advice for Executives on Transitioning from Intense Careers to Fulfilling Next Seasons*

ISBN-13: 978-1545146040

1. Retirement

2. Executives

3. Transitions

4. Coaching

5. Aging Workforce

*Book Design: Scattaregia Design*

First edition published 2017 by My Next Season (v2)

Printed in the United States of America

# Your Next Season

**Advice for Executives on Transitioning from Intense Careers to Fulfilling Next Seasons**

# Contents

# About the Authors

**Dr. Leslie Braksick** has spent her career advising and caring deeply about her clients, who lead many of our nation's largest companies. Leslie is now in her first Next Season.

**Dr. Bill Innes** has spent his career as a corporate executive, leading others, developing and delivering ambitious strategies on behalf of his former employer, ExxonMobil. Bill is in his third Next Season.

Both share their observations on how critical and fragile the transition from corporate leader to "retirement" is, how often it happens unwell, and the prolonged, sometimes unrecoverable consequences of that.

Through this book, Leslie, Bill, and their MY NEXT SEASON colleagues and clients invite you into the important conversation and exploration of executive transitions out of corporate life, which set the stage for future, joy-filled Next Seasons.

Complete bios for Drs. Braksick and Innes may be found in the back of this book.

# Dedication

........................

For **Steve Simon** and **Liam McGee**,
whose Next Seasons were too short.

# To Everything There Is a Season

*To everything there is a season,*
*and a time to every purpose under heaven:*

*a time to be born and a time to die,*
*a time to plant and a time to uproot,*
*a time to kill and a time to heal,*
*a time to tear down and a time to build,*
*a time to weep and a time to laugh,*
*a time to mourn and a time to dance,*
*a time to scatter stones and a time to gather them,*
*a time to embrace and a time to refrain from embracing,*
*a time to search and a time to give up,*
*a time to keep and a time to throw away,*
*a time to tear and a time to mend,*
*a time to be silent and a time to speak,*
*a time to love and a time to hate,*
*a time for war and a time for peace.*

*What do workers gain from their toil? I have seen the burden God has laid*
*on the human race.*

*He has made everything beautiful in its time. He has also set eternity*
*in the human heart; yet no one can fathom what God has done from*
*beginning to end.*

*I know that there is nothing better for people than to be happy and to do*
*good while they live.*

*That each of them may eat and drink, and find satisfaction in all their toil—*
*this is the gift of God.*

*I know that everything God does will endure forever; nothing can be added*
*to it and nothing taken from it.*

> *— Ecclesiastes 3:1–14*
> *from the King James Version and*
> *the New International Version*

# Foreword

............................

THE BEST LEADERS HAVE A KNACK FOR SEEING AROUND CORNERS. They have intense curiosity, are energized by change, see potential in the unknown. They can dive deep into data, or ask a question so open-ended that it paints the sky a more provocative shade of blue.

Surprisingly, even leaders like this don't always know what to do for an encore. When it comes time to retire—or, to put a finer point on it, when it's time to close one of the longer and traditionally more visible chapters of life—even the visionaries among us aren't sure what to do next.

It's understandable: we've tended to view retirement as an end, rather than as the Next Season of purpose and possibility. Yet this is precisely the moment when we can have tremendous impact, unleashing our gifts in new ways that improve the lives of others.

In my role at GE, one of my responsibilities is to oversee our talent pipeline and development efforts, including the transformational Crotonville leadership experiences we offer employees throughout their careers. These experiences are often life events, full of a-ha moments and powerful breakthroughs that help employees pursue a future far brighter than any they'd imagined for themselves.

When Leslie Braksick asked me if I would contribute a few thoughts to these opening pages, I was eager to do it. She and I share a belief that learning, discovery, invention—and *reinvention*—should be lifelong practices; there's no reason any of that has to end at retirement. In fact, your Next Season can actually be a great time to up your game.

I first met Leslie some years ago when she was interviewing GE Chairman and CEO Jeff Immelt for another book she was working on at the time, *Preparing CEOs for Success: What I Wish I Knew*. Based on those early conversations, we invited Leslie and her colleague Bill Innes in to work with some of our leaders as executive coaches. Then, after she launched MY NEXT SEASON with Mark Linsz, we retained her and her team as trusted advisors, helping our retiring executives contemplate life's proverbial third act.

Leslie's empathy and humility are remarkable, enabling her to connect with people from all walks and show them where their deep, sometimes forgotten passions might lead. Leslie and her team have been a tremendous help to many of my colleagues, and to me.

So what's next for you? If you are approaching retirement, or have already retired, remember that you are accountable to different "stakeholders" now—family, friends, yourself—in a whole new way. And your success metrics are probably due for some reimagining as well.

As Leslie and co-author Bill Innes note, "The only thing defining success in your Next Season is that you feel joy, purpose, peace, and excitement about how you choose to spend your time." Does that feel a little uncomfortable and open-ended, especially compared to decades of deadlines and quarter closes? I hope so!

Change, ultimately, is a matter of learning and adapting. And it often requires a mindset shift. But you may be more prepared than you realize. Think of all those finely honed capabilities you've developed: your ability to influence, to make tough calls based on instinct and judgment, to rally a team around a vision, to move an organization, to spot talent and help others rise higher. The world needs capabilities like that now more than ever.

I encourage you to think broadly and deeply about what you may yet achieve. Use this book as your guide.

*Your Next Season* is an investment in a future you may not yet have imagined for yourself, but one that awaits you with open arms and untold promise.

*Carpe diem.*

**Susan P. Peters**
Boston, Massachusetts
May 2017

......................................................................................................

*Susan P. Peters is Senior Vice President, Human Resources, General Electric Company, responsible for GE's global workforce of 300,000. From 2007 to 2013, she served as GE's Vice President, Executive Development and as Chief Learning Officer.*

# 1

# Out of the Frying Pan

*Imagining a future that is truly your own*

WHEN YOU ARE IN THE HEAT OF THE BATTLE as a corporate executive, it's hard to imagine what's on the other side. Your life is consumed with phone calls and meetings, travel and dinners out, presentations, explanations, expense reports, budgets, and on and on. There are endless demands for your time and opinion. It is a relentlessly *busy*, all-consuming lifestyle.

The higher you are in your company, the more command your company has over your non-work time and commitments. Add your family obligations, and you have a schedule that is long on appointments and short on time. It is hard, if not impossible, for executives to commit to non-work leadership opportunities due to their unpredictable schedules. Even close friendships tend to have a work connection.

After many years of this intensity, the word "retirement" can make a seasoned executive experience real anxiety as the implications sink in. *What will I do with all of that time?*

For many, the fears are very real, and run very deep. For everyone, the thoughts and concerns about "retirement" are deeply personal. What will I do *every day?* Who will I interact with? How will I stay mentally sharp? How will I stay "in the game" of business, if I want to? What will my relationship with spouse and children be like when I am home so much?

After a lifetime of being part of a huge, fast-moving machine, it is painful to imagine a future without portfolio or primary affiliation. *Who am I when I am no longer executive of such-and-such?* It is natural to dwell on what *was* rather than what *will be.*

......................

For others, the anxiety may be somewhat delayed. Some eagerly count the days until their last official presence in the office, and are excited about finally having time to detox, decompress, focus on their health, and perhaps join a board or two. For these folks, the impact of the transition comes a bit later, and the unexpected feelings often are even harder-hitting. Questions like "Am I still relevant?" and "Am I still on the list?" grow with each passing week.

Your renaissance happens, though, when the focus shifts away from a life constructed around career *productivity* to one oriented to *purpose*. It is like going to HD full-color video after decades of black and white. It is your opportunity to transition from a season of *getting* to one of *giving*—from a season characterized by *gaining* personal value to one of *giving* personal value. Your new possibilities are endless.

The key, though, is getting there—navigating that transition. That's where it all starts. That's what this book is all about.

......................

When the transition happens well, amazing things follow. But if the transition happens poorly, it can be unrecoverable. Some executives never get beyond the transition and, as a result, they are never all they can be in their Next Season. Most can name friends, colleagues, or relatives who experienced real stress or worse from their transition and from the absence of finding a suitable Next Season.

Some executives are angry if the exit comes sooner than expected. Others suffer from disappointment if they were not asked to stay longer. After so many years of personal sacrifice and commitment, many expect more from their exit package than they receive so, as a result, they cut off contact with the very people with whom they had valuable relationships for decades of their professional life. And some executives are simply lost, never able to find something on the other side that they love as much as their work.

I recall attending the retirement of a very successful colleague who had made a huge contribution in his corporate career. Steve was one of the "greats." A colleague who spoke to him in the receiving line of his retirement party offered heartfelt congratulations and shared that he must feel so proud of all he had achieved and the impact he had. The colleague was taken aback when Steve replied, "This is the worst day of my life." And he meant it.

Despite an incredibly happy 48-year marriage to a woman he adored and a beautiful family in which he took great pride and enjoyed sharing time with, *his life was his work*. And without it, he felt no identity, no purpose. Thirteen months later, while home alone, Steve suffered a massive heart attack.

Steve's death inspired not only this book in part, but the founding of MY NEXT SEASON, a company whose sole purpose is to help executives transition from careers of intense productivity to lives of purpose . . . and realize fulfilling Next Seasons.

Steve's experience was tragic, but not unique. It is hard for executives to switch gears after decades of dedicated service to an employer. It is precisely why transitioning is not like flipping a switch. Rather, it is a process.

...........................

Concern about "what's next," and your identity once you leave your corporate role, may well describe you. But take heart: you are not alone in your concerns, nor your experience.

The transition process can be especially challenging if your exit was not initiated by you. While it may not ease your unhappiness, it's important to remember that decisions are often driven by a corporate agenda for strategic talent, cost reduction, etc., and not by evaluation of you as an individual. Sometimes it is simply done with the company's need to retain or promote younger talent felt to be critical to the firm's long-term future. That may not make you *feel* any better, but as a likely shareholder of the company, or person who wants to see the company succeed, it is important to separate the company's decision from your own valuation.

The circumstances of your leaving do not define how you move forward. In fact, you have to ensure they don't. Perhaps it is best to allow that dynamic chapter of your own book to close, and begin writing the next chapter, for which you are both author and main character. The next chapter is *Your Next Season*.

And your Next Season is brimming with possibilities! So, lean in and keep walking forward. Your best days are still ahead!

# 2

# The Art of Transitioning Well

*It's not about endings, but beginnings*

M ANY BOOKS HAVE BEEN WRITTEN about "the big R," about how to retire successfully. With young-in-age and young-in-life executives transitioning out of companies today, it is no longer a story about the "R" word, but rather a story about *transitioning*. It is not about endings, but beginnings. And the least-talked-about, yet most important part of that is the transition itself: bridging from your current state to your future state, and ensuring that it happens well.

As companies have assumed control over retirement timing, lead times are growing shorter and executives are finding themselves in transition well in advance of their expectation—or preference. These shortened windows create abrupt endings for a generation of leaders who have sacrificed for their employers for most of their career.

One important question to answer about your transition is what to take with you and what to leave behind. Much of what you have learned/perfected over these past decades needs to be front and center with you on the journey, but you also have acquired a lot of *baggage* that adds weight and is of little help on this next leg.

Three examples of *baggage* include living by your Outlook calendar, neglecting your health, and defining yourself through work:

1. ***Living by your Outlook calendar.*** Somewhere along the way, Outlook went from being a convenient system of calendar appointments to the Ruler of the Executive Universe. Flexibility was unknowingly traded for an invisible electronic dictator who tells you where you must go, when, and with whom. For most executives, Outlook schedulers have more say over where you spend time than you do, and family/children are a distant third or worse in the pecking order of influencing whether or not you can attend something. (*When did THAT happen?!*)

   This is not to suggest that electronic scheduling is a bad thing, because it isn't. But recognize that for many executives, everything they do is determined by those who have control over scheduling, versus where the executive wants to spend time and who to spend it with. Your Outlook calendar is not just something you leave behind in your transition—it's a thing you *want* to leave behind, though it may feel intimidating at first.

   One of the biggest transition adjustments is regaining control over how you spend your time. It will feel like a burden at first, and a little daunting: "How will I spend my time every day?" But with that question comes immense power over your time. The freedom to choose what you do with your time is one of the most liberating and enjoyable aspects of your Next Season.

2. ***Neglecting your health.*** The demands of your job may have forced you to adopt some personal habits you now must leave behind: inadequate sleep, excess food or drink, and too little exercise. Late nights, early meetings, relentless travel, alcohol-and-carb-rich dinners out with clients and

colleagues—they all add up. Your body needs to detox and be readied for the next leg of your journey.

Most working professionals (and parents of young children) have learned to function on too little sleep and meals on the run. They skip exercise regimens and other activities of personal benefit and pay an invisible price that becomes increasingly problematic with age.

Leave behind the pattern of "getting by." Deliberately schedule meetings, breakfasts, calls, and flights during hours that do not compromise your sleep. Make—and stick with—an exercise routine that helps ensure your physical limitations will not hinder your Next Season plans and dreams. Abandoning prescription sleep aids and other medications will help your mind and body return to its natural, healthier state.

3. *Defining yourself through work.* You probably have become comfortable with being known by your title and corporate role. But you were never just that, nor was your impact made just because of that aspect of your being. As you transition out of your corporate role, you will be taking the very best parts of yourself with you.

So leave behind metrics tied to productivity and getting things done because of your title and authority. Instead, spend your time generously with people you enjoy and care about, and do things that interest you and bring you joy.

Do not concern yourself with whether or not you accomplished enough today! The days of corporate scorekeeping and receiving respect because of your accomplishments are over, and that is to be celebrated. It doesn't mean you don't keep score, nor that you will no longer be respected. It means you keep score only for things that are important to you.

*Scorekeeping.* One executive, Tom, provided an example of healthy scorekeeping in his Next Season. He wants to visit every major league baseball park in America with his son after transitioning out as CEO of a large bank. Tom and his son both love baseball and enjoyed attending games together when his son was younger. Tom realized this shared tradition had evaporated when his son left for college. Between Tom's climb up the corporate ladder to Chairman/CEO and his son being away at school, the father-son baseball outings became history. Today, Tom is monitoring the achievement of his visit-all-the-parks goal, but the larger goal is recommitting *time* to his son while doing something they both love. It's as much about reconnecting and rekindling their relationship as it is about visiting every stadium.

"Visit 100 by 100" is a different goal for John, who plans to visit 100 countries before he turns 100. John transitioned out of his corporate role as Chairman/CEO of a company with a large international footprint and realized he had already visited 75 countries. So he thought it would be fascinating to get to 100 before his last season, and at the time of this writing he had just four to go! Scorekeeping in this sense is OK—because it is enabling something that has a larger personal purpose and is important to John after spending most of his adult years traveling in service to his company and leadership responsibilities.

Another executive with whom we worked retired from a major operating leadership role at the time of his company's mega-merger. Directors and the soon-to-be-minted CEO encouraged Brian to consider a big job in the combined entity, as he was a highly respected leader and executive. Instead, he opted to sail from the US to Australia, his home country, over many, many months, with his wife of many, many years. He shared that:

*Men die young in my lineage and I don't want to spend another day away from the person I love most in the world, doing the thing I enjoy most in the world, that will deliver me to the rest of the people I care most about in the world.*

Tom, John, and Brian each set goals and kept score for things that mattered to them. This is often a strategy to bridge for a life spent scorekeeping while transitioning from *busy* to *meaningful*.

Another important takeaway related to transitioning to a meaningful Next Season is to let go of any "guilt" or feeling of insufficiency if you have days where you simply enjoy time with those you care about, get lost in a novel or fly fishing, sail to Australia, or simply enjoy some fresh air and sunshine. Some days will be spent fulfilling a personal goal, while others will blend one into another, because they can . . . and because there is no externally imposed monitoring of activity and productivity.

## What Makes This So Difficult?

One thing that makes transition difficult for the current generation of senior executives is the extreme corporate loyalty they feel and have proudly embraced. If you consult a dictionary for a definition of corporate loyalty, you would see the photos of this generation of executives with descriptors including: *willing to do whatever it takes, devotion, faithfulness, allegiance, trustworthiness,* and *dependability.* You would see pages of examples like *willing to work endless hours because that's what it takes…, taking calls 24/7, having phones at ears during children's sporting events, interrupting family time and shortening vacations to accommodate business needs, traveling across multiple time zones in a single week,* and *enduring unending stress from living in the world of confidential information not able to be discussed with others.*

For this "live-to-work" generation, "loyalty" was a requirement to succeed at the highest levels. Defined by their jobs, these folks did whatever it took to be in full service to their companies and their roles. Perhaps that describes you. You may feel extremely tied to your company and cannot imagine life without this responsibility and identifier. That is what makes retirement and transition so hard.

One executive we interviewed, George, was Chairman/CEO of a global company. With only three months' notice, the board decided to hand his role to his successor—a full two years before George expected to transition out. He was upset and felt disrespected after a selfless career with the company, including multiple international relocations with his family and weekly global travel and commitments. He reflected:

> *It felt like a death sentence. I was shocked and disappointed, with no plan in place for what to do next. I wish I had spent more time thinking about and preparing for the transition. I needed to sever my emotional relationship with the company, because I disagreed with many changes they were making. I also disagreed with the views of my successor. Frankly, I needed to accept that I was no longer in control and separate emotionally from actions being planned under my successor's regime. It was eating me alive. I needed to preserve myself.*
>
> *I realized that I needed to focus energy on my family and personal relationships—immediately—because I had shortchanged them during my career. I realized I could do this only by focusing on my future and not holding on to my past.*

Today, George is on the other side of the transition, and he notes:

> *I am happier than I have ever been. I thoroughly love being in charge of my own time and schedule. I have more time for my private life, children, and grandchildren. I have found purpose in my church volunteer work and the other organizations I have chosen to get involved with. Achieving happiness necessitated my letting go—really letting go—and I realize now that part of what made that hard, was that I had nothing in place to grab on to.*
>
> *I highly recommend that executives plan early for their transition—contemplate their relationships and time expenditure—even while they are still working. Think about hobbies, nonprofit interests. Don't wait until you leave your job to think about getting involved in those things—because you just don't know when that end will come.*

Contrast George's experience with that of another CEO, John, who was informed over a year in advance of his board's timeline for transition. With the advance notice, John had time to adjust and plan for the change and commit to transitioning well, so his successor was set up for success. John comments:

> The relationships at work were the hardest things for me to leave behind. I had become so close to my team and colleagues over my 29 years with the company. It was so hard to walk away from them. However, retirement from my corporate role allowed me to rekindle relationships and emphasize time with my family, whom I had largely neglected in my ascension to bigger jobs in the company, all of which required extensive international travel.
>
> I was on a public board at the time of my transition, which was an essential part of transitioning into my Next Season. It allowed me to remain involved with the corporate environment in a way that would not compromise family time. Retirement allowed me to take up new hobbies such as fly fishing and take trips with friends, which I was never able to do with my work schedule and commitments. I became involved with my college alma mater and serve them using my skills and experience gained as a corporate executive.
>
> Job One for me in retirement was transitioning my identity and relationships from work to family, friends, and the boards I opted to go on in my Next Season. It required a mental shift on my part, a letting go, a grabbing hold.

Another executive of the live-to-work generation described his first day of retirement:

> It was the hardest day of my life. The silence from being off email lists, meeting requests, and phone calls, while welcomed intellectually, was deafening. I could not see beyond my blank calendar and imagined it would remain like this the rest of my life. I felt sick and tense from head to toe, and began to question who I was and what I would do the rest of my life.

Martha, a Fortune 50 executive, offered this insight:

*Many are afraid of retirement because they are losing a long-developed identity. It took me at least a year before I stopped telling people "what I used to do"—almost as though that somehow validated my worth. Establishing your new identity may feel uncomfortable at first, but it is a chance to redefine who you are, what matters most to you, and what you stand for. Take full advantage of it. Embrace the "new you."*

And Lori, the spouse of a client, offered her own account of the challenge of breaking free:

*Following my husband's retirement, I saw was how hard it was for him to shift his paradigm of how the day flows and where to focus. He was addicted to following the stock market and specifically, his former company. He would wake up to see the Wall Street opening bell, watch MarketWatch, and track the performance of his former company throughout the day. He would get depressed if the stock went down and become all knotted up about why, what should be done, etc.—as though he were still in charge. The stock price of his former company literally determined his mood for the day.*

*Mind you, a chunk of our net worth was tied up with that company's stock, so how it performed was important to us both. But to monitor it compulsively, as he had in his former season? No. It is so important that executives let go and let themselves break free in order to fully live into their Next Season.*

There are executives who report little anxiety on the front end of their transition, but confess concern about whether they will still be "relevant" and marketable if they don't commit to something right away. Our colleague Amy Baldwin, who has initial conversations with every MY NEXT SEASON client, shares this as a common phenomenon. Executives often *want* to take a break, but feel (self-applied) pressure that, if they are ever to do something *professional* again, they must to do it right away.

Our recommendation is to take time early on to prepare yourself "on paper" by having a bio, updated resume, and current LinkedIn profile—all with a current photo—so you are current and "ready to go" if/when an opportunity that interests you arises. It is important to maintain or initiate relationships that may help you bridge to opportunities that interest you. However, it is not necessary to commit to something right away. In fact, doing so often results in committing to what is merely *available* to you versus what is *compelling* to you. Transitioning well combines two things:

- Proudly acknowledging what you have accomplished during the main chapters of your life/career
- Finding comfort turning the page to your life's next chapter

*It is about transitioning from productivity to purpose,* looking ahead with hope and anticipation of what will come to define you in your Next Season and phase of life. It is also about letting go so you can be fully present in your Next Season.

Most executives spend the first half of their careers focused on learning, growing, and climbing the corporate ladder—while balancing heavy home commitments of young children and family. As work intensity increases, time for outside commitments decreases. The problem is that nonwork (outside) commitments rarely get added back in, so when it comes time to retire, executives feel as though they have nothing to transition to.

In truth, *it is these other connections that bridge the transition* for executives. These outside areas of interest provide structure for projects and part-time engagement, while the rest of your Next Season picture comes into focus.

So: invite hobbies back into your life while you are still running the corporate race. Increase time spent with family. Engage with a nonprofit whose cause speaks to your heart. Sometimes it requires you to try things to see what engages your heart.

Force yourself to expand your aperture of what defines and interests you. It will make a big difference when the time comes to make your corporate transition from productivity to purpose.

# 3

## The Pause

*Pausing is necessary for future progress*

A VERY IMPORTANT BUT OFTEN-OVERLOOKED STEP in the transition is *The Pause*. It is your space for focused thought and discernment about what's next. It is incredibly hard to ponder the future amid the busyness of everyday work life—which is why *The Pause* makes all the difference in your process of discerning what to do next.

*The Pause* involves taking the time—*making* the time—to contemplate, reflect, and dream. It requires setting aside time away from the noise and activity of your everyday life and just thinking about yourself, what you enjoy and don't enjoy, and contemplating what your Next Season might hold. Here are three things to consider during your Pause:

1. What have you always wished you had the time to do?
2. What activities over the past decades brought you the most joy?

3. If on the last day of your life, someone were to describe how you spent your Next Season, what words would you want to hear spoken?

***What will I do next?*** You have spent three or four decades in a profession, or series of professions, and prior to that, you invested years becoming educated, certified, and qualified to practice your profession for as long as you can remember. Since your work is what your life has been mostly about, how can you even imagine what to do next?

You likely know plenty of people who will generously dole out "helpful advice" on what you should do next—former colleagues, neighbors, relatives, friends. Such advice usually includes the "s" word: *should.*

Those intending to be helpful seem to have an abundance of should's for you: "You *should* go on a corporate board." "You *should* spend time with your children and grandchildren." "You *should* find a hobby." "You *should* focus on your health." "You *should* downsize." "With your experience, you really *should* . . ." It seems like everyone has a *should* to offer, but all that does is add another "s" word to your life: *stress.*

There is no place for *shoulds* when it comes to defining how to spend your time. Each person's life looks and feels different, based on personal needs and desires, life goals, constraints (personal, financial, health, geographic), gifts and interests, career experiences, connections/networks, etc. You don't need to accept someone else's view or advice. You are the best expert on you.

***Pause and reflect on what you feel called to do.*** You've worked hard and earned the right to think it through and choose what you want to do, what feels right to you, what brings you joy, where you want to make a difference in your post-corporate life. And remember: you're deciding only on what's next for you, not what's forever.

Karen, a Fortune 50 executive, found herself in transition, but not of her choosing. Here are her reflections and advice:

*When my company restructured, I found out that I would be transitioning sooner than planned. I still had some time to prepare, but I was afraid of what life would look like on the other side. My worst fear was waking up on the first morning after leaving and realizing I had nothing to do. It's terrifying to think of a life without any purpose or anything to look forward to. My advice:*

- **Take back control of your calendar.** *When my retirement came, I knew that I needed a pause to think about what I wanted to do. I didn't want to completely give up work. In my Next Season, I have the option to work, but I can also work on my own schedule. I needed a pause to put a plan together.*
- **Take advantage of a second chance with your family.** *I spend more time with my children and grandchildren now and even volunteer at my granddaughter's school. So, look for new opportunities to connect.*
- **Listen to others, but process the information on your own.** *Gather advice from friends and colleagues, network, and be open to opportunities—but filter them accordingly, to identify what you really want to do in your Next Season.*
- **Join an exercise class.** *It will keep you fit and provide a great way to make friends since you aren't going to the office every day.*
- **Rediscover an old hobby.** *I took a quilting class and finally learned how to use the sewing machine that had been gathering dust in my basement.*
- **Learn how not to be in charge.** *It's tough when you go from giving direction to being a participant. Let go of the frustration; it can actually be quite freeing.*
- **Envision what type of day will be fulfilling to you and bring you joy.** *Create that day by including a variety of activities that will make you excited to get out of bed every morning.*
- **Find a way to pay it forward.** *I really enjoy mentoring young executives, providing advice and guidance on their career and life goals. It's something I didn't have access to in the early stages of my career. Coaching some of the rising stars I've stayed in touch with has been a pleasure; I always walk away feeling energized.*

Each phase of your life is defined, governed, and enabled by so many factors that change: your physical and mental health, the health of your spouse/partner and children, the presence/care of aging parents, etc. Our eyes don't allow us to see around a corner, which is why thinking about your future as *seasons* is helpful—because seasons change.

As a result, this transition requires flexibility to honor the needs of others and adjust to shifting constraints as well as a commitment to discerning what's most important to you. Don't allow yourself to be artificially constrained by someone else's should's regarding what your retirement looks like. Rather, keep your aperture open wide, contemplating the unlimited possibilities.

For many people who have enjoyed success at work, the noise around them from well-intended people can be loud. The key is to listen hard for the whispers: the quiet voice of possibilities. Sometimes you alone are the whisperer.

Maybe it is reflecting on a book or article you read. Perhaps it is recalling a conversation with someone while you stood in line for something else. Perhaps it's a billboard that always caught your eye on your drive home from the airport. Maybe it's a long-ago connection to your past . . . something your grandparents or parents were involved in that you have always wanted to learn more about or get closer to. Maybe it's reading an alumni magazine and learning what a former classmate is doing.

***Listening to whispers and wonders are precisely what The Pause is all about—and what discernment looks like.*** You've earned the right to imagine possibilities. And those possibilities may be something as simple as rekindling your relationship with your spouse, repairing a difficult relationship with a child or sibling, or being physically present and more involved in the lives of your grandchildren.

Other possibilities might be more ambitious: learning a new language, starting a company, teaching a class, or giving lectures. Possibilities could involve formal mentoring, writing articles, or sharing your life story. Whatever it is, be generous with your personal acceptance for the simple. Embrace whatever brings you real joy. One executive, Richard, offered these thoughts:

········································································································

*My transition was somewhat of a shock. I was not prepared for life outside of my corporate job. You go from having 15 meetings a day and 100 people trying to get on your calendar to having absolutely nothing to do. It's a huge change and you have to prepare for it. My advice:*

- ***Plan your days.*** *You need to have more plans than just a broad generalization like "I want to travel" or "I want to play golf." What are you going to do when you wake up, and then the hour after that?*
- ***Think beyond the basics.*** *There are lots of advisors who can help you with your finances or your health in retirement. You need to think beyond that, however, and plan what you're going to do with your time as well.*
- ***Do something different.*** *Most people don't want to retire in the classic sense; they just want to be able to do something completely different. I started a second career as a coach and advisor so that I could use my skills, but in a new way.*
- ***Keep your company friends.*** *Just because you aren't working at your company doesn't mean that you can't still be friends with your coworkers. A lot of my colleagues have become my close friends, and I still see and talk to them regularly.*
- ***Try new things.*** *The best part about retiring is having the luxury of doing things I couldn't do before.*
- ***Spend time with your family.*** *As an executive, I had to miss a lot of important events in the life of my family. Retired, I had the time to become reacquainted with my spouse and witness all the milestones in my children's lives.*
- ***No executive assistant.*** *One of my most difficult adjustments was not having an executive assistant to book my travel and meetings for me. Everyday tasks became a little bit harder when I had to do it all myself.*

- *Take self-assessment tests.* Sometimes after doing one thing for so long, it's hard to even remember what your interests are outside of work.

It is important to answer some questions honestly—about what you enjoy/don't enjoy, what activities bring you feelings of joy/fulfillment, and what you'd just as soon leave behind. (A *Personal Inventory* can be extremely helpful at this juncture. At the back of this book, please see "Your Next Season Tools," *Personal Preferences Inventory*.)

One entrepreneur with whom we spoke was ready to leave behind the challenges of running his company and move on to new adventures. Still young and healthy, he opted to sell his creation and embark on a Next Season. Here is Barry's advice:

- *Embrace your faith.* Your Next Season can be a great time to focus on the direction and peace you can find in God. Be intentional about spending time exploring this area of life.
- *Don't feel guilty.* When I sold my company, I took on a more relaxed lifestyle. After a stressful job, a normal level of stress may seem like laziness, but it's actually very healthy. Be okay with slowing down!
- *Take where you want to live into consideration.* Think through the logistics and plan ahead. I haven't been able to do everything I wanted, because I couldn't sell my house immediately, which meant that I couldn't move automatically to a new life. I wish I had begun planning my physical geography and action plan sooner.
- *Become an expert at something new.* I decided I wanted to learn about market trading and make my own trades. I got some advice and coaching by others and did plenty of research online to better understand the subject. It was fun and it was different from anything I had ever done.
- *Go on adventures!* Get out of your comfort zone. Travel to a new place, go sailing, learn surfing, or do something crazy like hang gliding.

- **Stress can be addictive.** *So many people get adrenaline from the thrill of the hunt often associated with a busy corporate environment. Recognize that your frantic pace was your old norm, and allow yourself time to adjust.*
- **Focus on what you like and are good at.** *People might expect you to be on a board or volunteer at a museum, but if your passion is surfing or gardening or writing a memoir, then spend your time there. Go for it—on your terms. It is so freeing!*

The Pause cannot be rushed, and ideally it will span six months to a year. It's important to permit yourself the space and time to be messy in this process. Answers reached too quickly are usually less fulfilling than those that come after thoughtful reflection.

VIEWP◆INT

## The Reality of the Early Days

*John Thiel, Former Head*
*Merrill Lynch*

WHILE INTELLECTUALLY you can process and agree that three months is a long time, it's not long enough to make the switch from 14 meetings a day to none. And it's also not long enough to get things in motion, especially when you take the needed pause. Things simply take a long time, and reconciling the need for a break, with the need to occupy your time, doesn't come easily nor naturally.

While there is peace and joy from stepping away from the craziness of the executive life, the resulting silence can be deafening and the absence of externally imposed activities, jarring. Everything you try to do simply takes longer. It's a hard reality to adjust to. In fact, it feels like everything moves at a snail's pace, compared to what you are used to and what you just walked away from.

When you are going through this in the early months, there are natural emotions that, while part of the process, feel incredibly unfamiliar. You are used to leading, making decisions, and having people listen and follow those decisions—but suddenly, there are no followers, and you feel irrelevant. You worry that people are going to forget about you and about what you did, despite your being told, often, that folks at your former company are still feeling the void left by your absence and trying to adjust to life there without you.

It's hard to reconcile it all, really. It's hard to see former colleagues suffer, and it's hard to no longer "protect and defend." My message to future peers-in-transition: expect the early months to be hard, and be gentle with yourself as you navigate through them. It's all part of the process—but the process is not always easy.

My second piece of advice: be intentional about involving your spouse early in the process. As executives, we are used to getting our own way. Participative decision processes do not come naturally. Once you step away from your corporate life, you are still playing the game of life, but your event has gone from an individual sport to a team sport, and you have an equal partner to help you decide what plays to run and when. It's an adjustment. It requires a lot of listening and a behavior change relative to how you have operated successfully for decades.

The advice I received and heed: *be patient; embrace the importance of getting/feeling physically well first; and focus on reconnecting with people attached to things of interest to you*. That includes your spouse. In my case, I have been nominated for two boards, which is part of what I was hoping to do in my Next Season . . . but even that process is slow relative to what I am used to. And so, I have created shorter-term projects as I lay track for longer-term things like boards or other leadership roles.

My final observation: navigating the transition with the support and friendship of Leslie helped me so much.

It is guidance I sought and benefited from greatly. I am glad I did not try and go it alone. Her experience with so many details of a transition like mine remains invaluable as I progress to my Next Season.

## Will You Be "On Board"?

The instinct of many executives as they transition from their corporate role is to "go on a board." Some love the idea of keeping a foot in the corporate world, and being part of the governing body of an organization sounds interesting and exciting. Or so it seems at first.

When executives contemplate the details of securing a board seat and performing its duties—particularly a public company board—the excitement quickly wanes. They quickly realize that . . .

- They will be traveling/participating in multi-day meetings four to six times per year on dates set by the company (irrespective of their availability/ personal calendar).
- They will participate in committee calls between board meetings.
- They will review plans/financials/other documents sent with little lead time to study prior to meetings (while still being expected to have insightful commentary on these documents).
- They must invest time to understand the details of what is shared, but, out of respect for management/board boundaries, exercise restraint from getting into the details (the very place where they spent their careers).
- And there will be the hotels, early flights, scheduling, etc.

Suddenly, it all sounds a lot more like *work* than it sounds like *your Next Season!*

One colleague felt certain he was going to pursue board work after retiring from his operating company CEO position. But he was deterred by several factors:

1. Liability exposure increases every year; the impact is not so much financial (usually mitigated by insurance) but in the standards of due diligence that demand ever-closer involvement and attention to detail.
2. Time demands during periods of change in corporate structure or leadership can become extremely onerous and not at a time of one's choosing.
3. A significant proportion of board time is taken up with the process and administration of corporate governance, which is not intellectually challenging.
4. The relationship between boards and management is becoming more impersonal and distant with the increasing demands for independent oversight.

And so, while board service/directorship is precisely the right answer for some, for others, it is not. In addition, board seats on public companies are hard to get.

VIEWP◆INT

### About Public Board Directorship

*Deborah Dellinger, Director of External Engagement*
*My Next Season*

*SURPRISINGLY FEW NEW DIRECTORS are elected to public boards each year.* According to the Spencer Stuart Board Index, the number remains stable around 350 new board appointments annually over the past few years. However, only one-third of those are first-time board directors. The small number of board seats available each year is due, in part, to the lack of turnover, with board tenure averaging over 8 years, mandatory retirement ages rising (if they exist), and board size hovering at 11.

*Boards are generally most interested in retired CEOs/ COOs, financial executives, and leaders with global business experience.* The board wish list for new directors, in priority order: women, active CEO/COO, retired CEO/COO, minorities, finance executives, those with global leadership experience and orientation, and technology. There is a trend to look for active execs who are one or two layers below the CEO but are running a P&L and are (or were) acting in a role as a CEO.

*The single best path to a board nomination is recommendation by current board members.* This comes from a PricewaterhouseCoopers study. Fully 87% of boards reported using board member recommendations to recruit. The study also listed leads from management and, interestingly, searching public data sites—think LinkedIn—to identify potential board members.

*Boards today are concerned with many issues:* risk, cybersecurity, activist investors, global economies, and politics. Today's directors spend an average of 250 hours per year on board work and are expected to meet with employees and investors, tour company facilities, and serve on several committees. Most of the work happens outside of the board meetings—preparatory reading, committee work, and government compliance take much of the time—and all this is in normal times, with no crisis happening. To convey this numerically, in 2016:

- There were 345 new directors—1/3 first-time, 1/3 female (32%), 15% minority, 12% investors. Only 4% of boards have term limits, although many more are considering this.
- Director tenure averages 8.3 years, with average tenure reported as between 6 and 10 years.
- 73% of boards have a mandatory retirement age—average 72 years—and 39% have a retirement age of 75 or higher.

## It Takes Strength to Pause

Each time people ask, "What will you do after you leave your company role?" your commitment to taking *The Pause* is tested. Beware of giving a definitive answer right away to that question. It suggests that you may have side-stepped *The Pause* to just "check the box," versus truly taking the time to allow yourself to "not know what is next."

Don't be afraid to respond to that question this way: "I am contemplating several different possibilities, and sometime in the next six months or so, we'll both know which one(s) I opted to choose!" Though it may not feel like it, it is okay to not know what is next right away. In fact, it takes great strength and wisdom to allow yourself *The Pause*.

Taking time to step back and consider what you enjoy/don't enjoy helps to ensure you don't default to perpetuating only what you know and have always done. That may not be what you truly love, nor what you are truly purposed to do.

Charlie, a former corporate CEO, offers the following reflection and advice:

........................................................................................

*I was not ready to be done working when my company asked me to retire, so I began to look for opportunities to work in the corporate setting even after retirement. I wanted to do something truly new and different, so I joined boards in industries that interested me, but in which I did not have a lot of experience: places I could find opportunities to learn, work, and grow. I wasn't yet done with "corporate" and boards were my way to fuel that continued interest and passion. It was (and still is) where I felt I could contribute the most. My advice:*

- *Make the best use of your time and realize that retirement is not your last transition. It is instead the beginning of a series of transitions for which you need to prepare.*
- *Find things that you are interested in and in which you have skill and expertise. If you can determine what those subjects are, you can use them to have a great retirement.*
- *Pause, then plan. I didn't know what I wanted to do immediately, so I took a summer to pause and begin to wrap my mind around the future. Planning ahead is key because these decisions are important ones.*

- **Talk with people who have already transitioned.** *They have great advice, and their wisdom has significantly benefitted me during my transition.*
- **Listen to your spouse and family.** *If I'd been a better listener, I would have been able to accommodate their needs better and sooner.*
- **Find a strong financial advisor.** *Your finances are crucial in making your transition a smooth one.*

Retirement gives you the freedom to manage your own time and priorities, and to discover what those priorities are. Don't let that gift go to waste.

## What About Consulting?

An attractive route we have seen many executives pursue is consulting. Some opt to hang their own shingle, whereas others connect with an existing firm doing work that would benefit from their skill set, relationships, or domain expertise. Some benefits of consulting include:

- Much more control over your schedule. Consulting tends to be episodic, with a clear project beginning and ending.
- More variety in the work you do.
- Focus on business issues in an efficient and effective manner.
- Developing close working relationships with colleagues and clients.
- The opportunity to get into management/operating issues, which is familiar and enjoyable for those who have spent their careers there.
- Drawing on specific work or leadership experience and helping others.

Executives have found consulting to be a fascinating opportunity. Consulting brings privileged access to understand the essence of very different businesses. It also enables development of very personal relationships with some remarkable and talented people across different industries, geographies, and businesses.

If you are most comfortable with projects or structure, think of *The Pause* as your first pre-transition project. Like any other project, it requires time, thought, patience, and intentionality. It requires a goal and an end point. In this case, "the project" consists of giving yourself the time and space to contemplate, dream, dialogue, and explore. Try on many possible hats and see which one(s) fit you and tug at you to wear longer.

Randal, former CEO of a large private company, took exception to the word "retirement" and stressed the importance of seeking things outside of your normal routine/lifestyle:

*"Retirement" isn't a realistic word anymore. You just move on to the next exciting phase of your life. After 25 years at the same company, I reached a ceiling. Now I'm spending my time on new endeavors that I find just as fulfilling as anything I've ever done. I'll never really "retire." My advice:*

- *Find your path. When I was beginning my Next Season of life, I was optimistic about moving forward, but I didn't know which path to take. Finding that path was a three-year journey, but now I'm realizing my potential in amazing ways that I wouldn't have dreamed of before.*
- *Cherish your opportunity to reset. There are few times in life where you get a completely clean slate, so make sure to use it to your full advantage.*
- *Discover what you're good at and pursue activities in those areas. I know I have a gift for orchestrating and cultivating talented people. I now serve in leadership roles at not-for-profits that can use this skill.*
- *Work long-term with trusted advisors. It can shape your life in new and unexpected ways. After transitioning, I got involved with The Halftime Institute, which is a faith-based organization that helped me discover a holistic life plan for my next chapter.*
- *Do some "low-cost probes." Engage with a number of organizations before you decide which ones you'd actually like to spend significant time working with.*

- ***Stay active.*** *With more free time, you have more time to exercise, so don't neglect your body. I work out with a personal trainer four days a week to keep in good shape.*
- ***Make time for your spiritual life.*** *If you are religious, set aside time to actively work on your faith. Serving at your church or synagogue, volunteering with faith-based ministries, or spending time with religious friends are all ways to grow spiritually.*
- ***Understand that this is just the next step in a longer journey.*** *Know that these are not your final life decisions, but just the next decisions in a series moving forward.*

*The Pause* is critical to discerning your call . . . where you are meant to be, and what you are meant to do in your Next Season. Take the time to do it well. Go slow at first to go fast later. It makes all of the difference later on.

**4**

# Essentials for the Journey

*Three things you need for this voyage*

WHEN YOU TRANSITION FROM A CORPORATE ROLE into your Next Season, you need three essentials for the journey: your health, openness to a newly defined purpose, and companionship. Ironically, each gets compromised as executives work hard to fulfill their corporate duties. Let's have a look.

### Your Health

As mentioned, many executives put their health on hold as they travel around the world, crisscrossing time zones, doing the business of the business. For growing companies, "crazy-busy quarters" turn into "crazy-busy years," and with success comes increased demand and pressure. It is not unusual for an executive to be taking meds for high blood pressure, high cholesterol, or prescription sleep aids to quiet their minds at the end of stressful days. Exercise time gets squeezed out by early morning flights and late meetings/dinners. Business dinners always include alcohol and seldom are heavy on greens or grains. And so the personal health of executives often suffers as they do everything in their power to give the company their best.

Living fully into your Next Season requires you to have the physical health to do so. This is a time in your life to spotlight this more than you may have done in the past. MY NEXT SEASON'S Medical Concierge, Dr. Jennifer Daley, offers the following wisdom.

VIEWP◆INT

## A Prescription for Your Health
......................................................................................

*Jennifer Daley, M.D., Medical Concierge*
*My Next Season*

AS AN EXECUTIVE, you've spent sleepless nights mentally preparing, planning, or worrying about big meetings, big decisions, and big initiatives. While it might seem that transitioning out of those roles would reduce overall stress, handing *over* these responsibilities and being unsure of "what's next" may still have you tossing and turning. Transitions, whether welcomed and well thought out or not, bring about stress—a natural response to this significant change and a busy life. Now is the perfect time to reset!

With travel, business dinners, and packed calendars, exercise and nutrition have often been forced to the bottom of the priority list. In my role as MY NEXT SEASON'S Medical Concierge, I meet one-on-one with clients to discuss specifics regarding family history, caretaking responsibilities, health and wellness concerns, and goals. Here are some of my prescriptive suggestions for creating a solid foundation for both nutrition and stress management.

### Really Eating Healthy

What *does* it mean to "eat healthy" today? Bookstore shelves are filled with countless approaches to eating: low-fat, low-carb, clean eating, juicing, vegetarian, etc. With so much confusion surrounding this question, here are my seven easy-to-follow recommendations for healthy eating:

1. Eat a minimum of 100 grams of healthy proteins each day (e.g., Greek yogurt, oatmeal, lean meats, fish, beans, and non-fat cheese).
2. Eat an unlimited amount of green leafy vegetables—adding fruit in moderation.
3. Avoid eating white carbohydrates (e.g., bread, rice, potatoes, pasta, processed foods).
4. Eat a moderate amount of non-saturated fats (e.g., olive oil, safflower oil, canola oil, nuts, and nut butters).
5. Drink eight 8-ounce glasses of water each day.
6. Read food labels carefully, noting grams of protein, carbohydrates, and fat. Avoid foods that have a high proportion of carbohydrates-to-protein or high levels of saturated fat.
7. See your doctor before starting any diet to ensure you are in good health.

### Really Managing Stress

Knowing methods to reduce stress is common. But putting them into action during a time of storm or flux is challenging! Instead of reaching for that glass of wine, cookie, or iPad, try these solid, time-tested techniques to restore a sense of calm and presence. Your ultimate goal: increasing the enjoyment of your life!

- Get outside and into nature
- Play music (listen or perform)
- Exercise
- Eat healthy, nutritious foods
- Relax into healthy sleep patterns
- Read or write poetry
- Spend time with animals—maybe it's the right time for a pet
- Connect with friends and family—nurture your relationships
- Laugh
- Light a scented candle
- Take up gentle yoga practice

- Meditate
- Join social groups through church, volunteering, hobbies, and sports

Whatever you choose to do next, health and wellness will be your biggest and most essential asset!

## Openness to Newly Defined Purpose

At your time of retirement, you are unlikely to have full clarity on your next act or "purpose." Part of the reason is that you have had no space to pause and contemplate alternatives, let alone road-test new possibilities. It's not that you are closed to newly defined futures. It's simply a lack of time and capacity to contemplate/invent a future before retirement arrives.

In Chapter 3, we spoke of the importance of *The Pause* to discern your next calling. Even if you continue working full-time, there are things you'd likely prefer not to repeat about your last job, whether it be pace, intensity, work content, role expectations, work environment, commute/travel requirements, geography, associates, etc.

Know that you have earned the right to be choiceful in what you do next. You are no longer fresh out of university with little work experience. Be open to what your gifts can enable you to do/work on, and listen to your heart about what makes you happy. Using "Your Next Season Tools" in the back of this book, or conversations with a Next Season Advisor, examine the many ways your gifts and skills can be applied elsewhere.

Be open to the possibilities. Be honest with yourself about what brings you joy, what makes you anxious, and how you would like to spend this important Next Season of your life.

## Companionship on the Journey

It is not unusual to have stressed relations—marital and/or family—by the close of your career, or to have few real friends outside of work. After years of missing events, taking calls and working while on family vacations, and living in a world of "confidential," it is hard to open up with others. It's no wonder that executives find themselves feeling alone and stressed—just at the time when they need friends most and a support system to bridge from old to new.

Socializing, which was so much fun and energizing at the beginning of your career, often becomes stressful and exhausting by the end. Thus, at a time when you most need friendships and companionship to help process your transition, these may be a scarce commodity. Here is some wisdom from My Next Season co-founder Mark Linsz.

VIEWPOINT

## Pausing and Reprioritizing: It Changed My Life

*Mark Linsz, Co-Founder & Senior Managing Partner*
*My Next Season*

IN MID-2012, I REFLECTED ON THE PAST FIVE YEARS. At the time, I was Treasurer of Bank of America and thought back on the financial crisis: the summer and fall of 2008, the Lehman and Merrill weekend, the bank downgrades, and capital raises. Our family had moved twice, from London to New York and from New York to Charlotte. Due to my daughters' school schedules, I was forced to commute for seven months with each move. My days were long and adrenaline-filled, and my nights were often sleepless as I mentally prepared for the next day or worried about what was next in the crisis.

While taking stock of my life and events of the prior years, I asked my wife Becky some questions. (With full disclosure, I feared hearing her answers.) I asked her: *How have I been doing as a husband and father? Am I spending enough time with you and our three girls? Am I around enough?*

I had trepidation about how she might answer these questions, but never expected the response she gave me. Becky confided that her concern for me was that I seemed to focus only on work and our family. She went on to say that she observed my having given up time with our friends and our extended family, and this concerned her. Seeing my work permeate my mind and mood, she felt strongly that I needed a hobby or something else to engage my heart, my mind, and my time.

That conversation with Becky was a wake-up call and a gift. I found myself unable to shake her words as I prepared to retire from Bank of America and co-found My Next Season. I knew Becky was right, but how could I fit more into my schedule? It felt nearly impossible.

I felt as though I always valued relationships. But in truth, I had taken no time in the preceding five years to build new relationships or to deepen old ones. I quickly recognized that was a part of my life I had to change.

I started by prioritizing time to establish and deepen relationships with several friends. It required my being intentional on scheduling an early breakfast, a coffee, or a drink in the evening. I had to make the time to spend time with people I cared about.

Shortly after that conversation with Becky, a friend that I reconnected with invited me to a golfing weekend. My gut reaction was swift: I did not have the time for golfing with friends. I had a full plate: the girls' schedules were full of things I needed to be present for, the to-do list at home was long, and frankly, I was a horrible golfer.

Thankfully, I consulted my best personal advisor (Becky) on the matter before responding to my friend. She strongly encouraged my going—and after much agonizing, I decided to say yes. I realized it was an opportunity to strengthen several relationships of importance to me and possibly build new ones.

The weekend was a blast. The relationships that formed that weekend are among my closest today. As a bonus, I realized that the challenging, invigorating sport of golf clears my mind as it helps me build relationships. (And I have gotten better, by the way!)

As I began to think about retiring, those friends helped me think through what I needed to add back into my life and to dream about my future again. In addition to an occasional round of golf, I joined a couple of not-for-profit boards and began mentoring a group of young business professionals on business and faith.

It has been three years since I retired, and I am so grateful to those friends who cared enough to help me through the transition and encourage me to pursue passions outside of work. My friends were there to help me think about finishing my job well and to help me process my own Next Season. And they continued to be there for me, to brainstorm and bounce ideas as I started My Next Season and as we grow it.

We've shared ideas, advice, challenges ... not to mention lots of great food ... and none of that would have happened, had I not paused to take stock of my life, be open to observations and coaching from someone who knew me well and loved me, and be open to reordering my life's priorities.

I still remember the feeling in my stomach as I asked those questions of Becky. I never thought her answer and encouragement would have such a profound impact on my future.

## Reaffirming and Strengthening Family Relationships

This also has its challenges. Most corporate spouses have coped with the demands of their executive spouse's business life by building an independent life of their own. A spouse who suddenly has time to spend together can at first be an intrusion. For example, a colleague shared that his wife told him that his consulting work rescued her from his "Eddie Syndrome" (remember Eddie, the dog on the comedy show *Frasier* who used to stare at him?). Apparently when he first retired, he used to stare at her with an expectant air—that they were going to do something together when she already had a full day!

Clients have told us they relied most on their spouse, or sibling, a former mentor, or a friend. Others rely on a Next Season Advisor who has walked in their shoes and can offer advice and a process for working through the transition. The important thing to recognize is that working through the transition is not a private activity—it is best done with the close companionship and conversation with people who know you and care about you, or who are professionally trained to help.

Fortunately, among the many upsides of transitioning is the opportunity to reset *everything* (except, of course, your age). This is the time to reclaim your life and relationships that matter to you and/or pursue new relationships you may not have had the bandwidth to enjoy in the past. It's a chance to eliminate unhealthy patterns that may have crept into your life.

With tremendous runway still ahead, you can redefine yourself and what you represent. It all starts with acceptance that you cannot and will not have it all figured out ahead of time—simply because you dedicated all of yourself to your job, advancing your career, fulfilling your employer's expectations.

Ted, a former Fortune 500 EVP, shared this perspective:

......................................................................................

*My company set their mandatory retirement age at 65, so I had to leave when I hit that arbitrary number. So-called "retirement age" has not caught up with people living healthier lives and being mentally active well into their eighties. I know that many people look forward to the traditional retirement age and having an abundance of time for golf and travel, but I enjoy the current balance I have between family and work. My advice:*

- **Try a new job** *if your company retires you before you are ready. Your experience, judgment, and energy are valuable.*

- **Stay fit and maintain a healthy weight.** *Run, walk, bike, hike, stay on the move!*
- **Combine business with meeting new people and diving into local life.** *People are fascinating—discover what makes them different and what motivates them.*
- **Arise at your best time.** *I get a surge of energy when I am going to work at 6:30 in the morning. Don't feel like you must give that up, just because the culture asks it of you.*
- **You can travel and work at the same time.** *Many people want to retire to travel, but I get plenty of opportunities to travel through my work. You just have to remain intellectually curious.*
- **Anticipate what you might like to do next.** *A slow transition into retirement or your next career might not happen. Be ready for a swift shift.*
- **Stay relevant.** *Many people think that once you retire, you are outdated, but you don't have to be. Do more than golf. Study, find a new job, volunteer, work in a political campaign, lecture, write, add value.*
- **"Experience never gets old."** *That was on a movie poster I saw. That is so true... 75 is the new 65. If you have something to give, use that skill. Your experience is no less valuable now that you are another year older.*

## What Have You Always Wanted to Do?

For the first time in a long, long while, your corporate employer is no longer determining what, where, or when you do everything. So, what have you always wanted to do? Who have you always wanted to share it with? What would bring joy to your life? This is a season of possibilities and often, in retirement, the answer to these questions is much more of a family decision—which requires inclusion of your spouse/partner in the decision.

Our client Liam transitioned from Chairman/CEO of a Fortune 100 due to a terminal illness that he had not widely disclosed. He had ready successors and was able to effect his transition with timing and grace rarely seen in the corporate world. Liam entered his Next Season with profound clarity and purpose and a desire to be as accomplished in his final season as he was in his prior.

Walking with his wife Lori hand-in-glove, Liam relocated her and their young boys close to his brothers and their families. He secured joint faculty appointments in law and business at his alma mater and began mentoring first-time CEOs of not-for-profits. Thus he shared lessons learned and advice with those who otherwise could not access a coach with his deep experience.

Liam channeled his energies productively and rewardingly, writing and publishing his reflections, sharing them in the classroom and with CEO mentees, and attending his children's events until his passing. The legacy from his Next Season is as meaningful as that from his decades of corporate career.

Liam's wife, Lori, offers the following Viewpoint.

## VIEWPOINT

### Leaving a Lasting Legacy

*Lori Tomoyasu McGee*

LEAVING A LASTING LEGACY may sound straightforward, but this goal can become even more impactful and meaningful when conversations are shared with a spouse, family member, or business partner, and the goal is achieved together.

For my late husband, Liam, who embarked on his Next Season while courageously battling cancer, discussions about his legacy and "Making a Difference" beyond his corporate success were enhanced by working with Leslie at MY NEXT SEASON. She was able to direct and counsel him about professorships at universities, and she helped orchestrate the capturing of his valuable experiences on paper and the strategic placement of articles in several business publications. Leslie was instrumental in keeping Liam's voice "alive" even after he passed.

This direction of "Making a Difference" also fueled me to focus on honoring his legacy by living Liam's motto— *Strive for Greatness*—a top leadership lesson he exemplified during his corporate career. Our family decided to partner with the National Cancer Center to help launch a brain tumor research fund in his honor.

Great strides have been made toward extended and improved quality of life for patients. I am also blessed to volunteer at that Center to assist families living with cancer throughout their journey. It brings me great peace and joy to know that I am working toward Liam's legacy of impacting others.

Even before his retirement, my husband and I engaged in thoughtful and intentional discussions about leaving a lasting legacy. If we had not done this, I would not have as much clarity about next steps. Liam had already left his mark as a visionary leader in business, but now, hopefully, his impact is helping those challenged by cancer or adversity.

I encourage everyone to thoughtfully think about furthering their lasting impact in their "Next Season" and to discuss this with someone who can help them achieve it. Perhaps their corporate platform was a mere springboard to leaving an even broader legacy beyond their corporate success—a broader legacy that could include conversations about supporting underrepresented students by sponsoring them or tutoring them, or mentoring someone who is starting their career in an industry where they have expertise, or possibly launching a new career with a particular social cause.

Keep moving forward, keep making a difference, and always *Strive for Greatness!*

*Lori was married to Liam McGee, one of the two people to whom this book is dedicated. Liam was the Chairman/CEO of The Hartford when he retired prematurely due to brain cancer. Determined to share his life lessons, he devoted his Next Season to mentoring first-time CEOs of not-for-profits, wrote and published white papers on business leadership topics, and secured joint faculty appointments in the Colleges of Business and Law at his alma mater.*

Another client, Andy, was told by his Fortune 50 employer that "it was time to retire" after 32 years in finance. He had served his corporate master for his entire career, but it was at the expense of his personal life: he had long given up his hobbies, and he had left not-for-profit boards for which he had personal passion. He rarely had time to attend the board meetings as he traveled to meet with global business leaders/CFOs, following the rhythms of his company's business.

Andy thought he had a few more years until retirement, but the company had other plans. Andy received a generous financial package and vested options and was told his retirement would be announced in six weeks, to take effect in three months.

Andy realized he had some repair work to do at home. His marriage had frayed due to his extended absences, plus work distractions when he was home. He needed his wife to be his partner on this difficult journey. She was the first person he told the news. He asked that they go through this transition process together, coping with what the changes meant and thinking through what they wanted to achieve together, and independently, in their next life season.

In their many hours in conversation, Andy did a lot of listening. To his great relief, his wife understood more than he gave her credit for. She felt the stress he was under at work and knew the unintended effect it had on his behavior at home and with her. She gratefully agreed to partner with him to discern what was next and approached the process as a Next Season for them both.

Andy also stepped up his networking. He reached out to friends, contacts at church, and elsewhere. He worked to rebuild what he had neglected for years. After several months and numerous conversations, Andy accepted an offer to join a not-for-profit board, chairing its Audit committee. He and his wife laid out a plan for some long-postponed travel together. And he resumed a daily exercise routine, which he had abandoned about seven years prior.

An experience with an Italian CEO and dear friend reminds me of Robert Frost's poem, *The Road Not Taken*. Giorgio had an advanced degree in chemistry and a brilliant career as a senior executive in the chemical industry. I visited him soon after he retired. As we walked along the bank of Lake Como, I asked what he had decided to do in retirement.

As a young man, Giorgio said he had two interests: science and literature. He decided to study science because it had better job prospects, which turned out to be an inspired choice. In retirement, he decided to return to his other interest and to his road not taken. He has become an authority on the Italian life and work of the Victorian English poet Shelley.

I was struck then, as I am now, by the power of the human spirit and the willingness of Giorgio and others like him to redefine himself in his Next Season. There is no end to the possibilities if you allow yourself to be truly open and discern your purpose.

Mark, a former Fortune 10 executive, did precisely that: he took the time to discern and live (more) into his purpose in his Next Season. Here are his thoughts . . .

........................................................................................................

*When my company and I decided my retirement time had come, I was ready. I'd spent 30 years with the same company, and there really wasn't any place left for me to grow. When you get that high in a corporation, open seats become harder to find. A number of head-hunters tried to recruit me to do jobs I'd already done, but I wanted to try some new things. My advice:*

- ***Get in sync with your spouse/partner.*** *My wife and I review our schedules every week and plan things together.*
- ***Talk with many people about your transition.*** *They'll often have great advice to share.*
- ***Stay in shape.*** *I try to exercise at least four times a week so this Next Season can be a healthy one.*
- ***Take your time before jumping.*** *This is your first chance in de-cades to look at your life and decide what you want to do. Use this as a chance to rescript your life and do something new. Executives tend to always be doing something, but sometimes it is best to push your pride aside and just reflect before moving forward.*

- **Consider returning to school.** *I'm a learner and an achiever, so I knew I wanted to go back to school after I retired. I'm currently undertaking a Masters in Divinity, and the experience has been extremely rewarding and refreshing after so many years in business.*
- **Use this time to give back.** *I volunteer with several organizations, including a prison ministry. I wouldn't have been able to serve during the height of my career. Sometimes the work is difficult, but the impact you're able to make is worth it.*
- **Do not define yourself solely by your work life.** *This is your best preparation for retirement. If you can maintain a focus in other areas of your life, then leaving your job doesn't seem like such a huge blow.*
- **Try something new outside your comfort zone.** *I've taken up beekeeping with some friends and love the new adventure.*
- **Your calendar is now your own.** *I'm still just as busy as I was at my old job, but now I get to decide 100% of what is on my calendar. I get to go to school, volunteer, serve on boards, and spend time with my family—all on my own time.*

# 5

# Reactivating Some Old Muscles

*Think about old relationships/connections
in new ways*

A S AN EXECUTIVE, NO ONE KNOWS BETTER THAN YOU that networking and reconnecting are extremely important. It's amazing how extensive your networks are: friends, family, current or former associates and clients, university connections, alumni networks, church friends. And friends of in-laws whom you met at "the wedding."

Thinking about these old relationships/connections in new ways is an important early activity in transitioning.

You really know a *lot* of people, and each of them is connected to other people, organizations, and interesting possibilities. In an era of social media, you can reach out very easily to just about anyone. So allow yourself to think outside the box.

Brenda, a former Fortune 100 executive, wanted to reinvent herself and leverage her experience and relationships into her Next Season. Here is what she had to share:

After 20 years in the financial services industry, the market crashed, and I realized I was ready to reinvent myself. I could have coasted to retirement, but I wanted to find a way to leverage my history as I explored something new. So I began to connect even more with people I considered to be advisors, as well as make new acquaintances. My advice:

- **Be deliberate and intentional.** I always told people to be deliberate and intentional with their lives, the choices, and the decisions they make. I decided I would do the same. It made the difference between taking the easy option that falls in your lap and charting a course toward something you truly want to experience or to offer.

- **Cast a wide net when considering your Next Season.** Talk to people outside your industry, because they might point you to exciting new opportunities. After two decades in the private sector, I transitioned into federal government to help establish customer-focused practices more common in the private sector. In doing that, I opened a whole new world of interest, productivity, fun.

- **Leverage your skill and experience.** Taking an honest and thorough inventory of your talents and gifts as well as what you enjoy is critical to the success of whatever you decide to do next.

- **Check your ego at the door.** The power of your position might be different in a second career, so be prepared to earn the respect of others who don't know your history.

- **Transitioning is not a quick jump, but a process.** Maybe a little more art than science. You need to be open, intentional, reflective, and communicative if you want to reinvent yourself. Really think deeply about your choices.

- **Try things you've never done before.** I had never run a marathon because the training takes so much time, but now I've run several and love the challenge.

- **Develop personal power instead of positional power.** Learn to separate yourself from your position and have confidence in the person you are, not just in what you do or what position you hold.

- ***Don't settle for the status quo.*** *I love the Mary Oliver quote, "What is it you plan to do with your one wild and precious life?" I ask myself that whenever I am tempted to settle for the status quo.*

Many executives, as they become more senior in their roles, find themselves with atrophied networking muscles. Meeting new people becomes entirely reactive and naturally embedded through meetings, conferences, and corporate events. Executives become accustomed to being sought out everywhere they go, so little proactivity is required to meet new people.

But this significantly changes when you transition out of a senior corporate role. You will have fewer regular instances of being the magnet to which all of the nails are attracted. Rather, you will need to use your magnetism to purposefully and intentionally connect with others.

Thankfully, most find their muscle memory to be excellent in this area. The same skills you used to "win friends and influence people" earlier in your career will return quickly, with tremendous payoff.

However, you just might need a few trips to the gym to activate those muscles again . . .

VIEWP◆INT

## Connecting Is the New Networking

*Kathryn Trice, Executive Associate*
*My Next Season*

WHAT'S YOUR REACTION when someone suggests that you "network"? For many, there is overwhelming dread—some from fear of the unknown, some from having to ask others for help. Networking seems so commonplace, and yet most are at a loss as to how to do it, or do it well.

Gary Frey, a friend to MY NEXT SEASON, knows a thing or two about networking. Gary has held impressive roles within large and small companies, including founding a brand consultancy firm, serving as Chief Impact Officer at a private equity/wealth planning firm, President of Bizjournals.com, and Senior Vice President at Bank of America.

But while his resume is extensive, it is anything but linear. Amidst much career success, Gary experienced great loss and hardship, from discovering his partner's embezzlement to losing the bulk of his net worth in a private equity firm. Gary has had to persevere and redirect his career path, with all its unexpected twists and turns. He is where he is today because of what he calls "connecting," as opposed to networking.

In 2015, while living in Ohio with no job on the horizon, Gary and his wife started planning next steps. Why not look for a job in Charlotte, NC, where they desired to live? So, Gary traveled to Charlotte, not necessarily to "network," but in his mind, to *reconnect* with friends—and hopefully build new relationships. Gary began by asking friends to help him "make some meaningful connections."

During his two weeks in Charlotte, he ended up having 30 meetings. As impressive as that was, Gary ended up revisiting Charlotte for two more 2-week stints, and set up another 60 meetings. On the last day of his third trip, he received a job offer.

Gary's "connecting" was essentially *strategic networking*. Gary suggests the following points to achieve your own smoother, more effective connecting/networking process:

- *Expand your network. As extensive as your personal net-work may be, it is never big enough.*
- *You need to connect with other connectors, so list personal contacts who know you, and who could potentially connect you to others. (From the 20 people Gary initially contacted in Charlotte, he was able to connect to others he didn't know, who in turn connected him to still others, to generate 90 meetings in a 6-week span.) If you lack your own network, seek help from a trusted friend who does have a network.*

- **Update your LinkedIn profile** with your most relevant work experience and a current, high-quality profile picture. Often, people you meet will first check out your LinkedIn profile—to get the gist of your background—and to see what you look like.
- **Email your personal contacts.** Keep it brief and to the point. Mention your interests/strengths and thoughts on what you see yourself pursuing, so your contacts will have to think outside any box they may have put you in. Like this—
    - "As you know, I have been <insert positions held most recently> and am looking for the next thing. Here are a few things I'm looking for . . ."
    - "Also, here is my LinkedIn profile <insert link> if you or someone else would like to know more about my experience."
- **Follow up with a phone call** if a week or two passes without hearing from your contacts. If need be, leave a message asking to get together for coffee/lunch/drinks. Ask for 30 minutes of their time.
- **Make it easy for those you are meeting.** Go to them. Pay for their coffee/breakfast/lunch. (Dinner is often off the table because people want to be with their families, though meeting for a drink after work might work.)
- **Don't let yourself be pigeon-holed.** If you see people limiting their search for you, based on your previous work experience or the job they last knew you had, it is up to you to reshape the conversation. Share your vision for what you are thinking career-wise, as well as your strengths. (For Gary, it had been 10+ years since he had been in Charlotte, and his contacts knew him as a marketing guru. They didn't know of his broader experience, working with high-net-worth clients. He shared his vision to reshape the conversation.)
- **Know your audience.** Every city is different. Is your city a breakfast city? Do people wear suit and tie? It is always better to err on the side of caution and be over-dressed, rather than too casual. Business casual is often a safe bet.

- ***Never miss an opportunity, even a doubtful one.*** *When a friend/contact suggests you meet with one of their contacts, always do so, even if you don't think it will serve you. You never know what will come from it! (Gary was hesitant to meet with a few contacts along the way, but one of those uncertain contacts eventually led to a job offer.)*
- ***Personal introductions to new contacts are worth their weight in gold.*** *One of Gary's personal contacts suggested he meet with one of theirs, so Gary asked if they'd be willing to make an introduction on his behalf (call or email). Gary also offered to send his contact an email outlining what he was looking for along with the link to his LinkedIn profile, so his contact could forward this email directly.*
- ***State your "ask" early in the conversation.*** *Don't directly ask for a job, but rather share your interest, work history, passions, strengths. Make it clear why you're there and don't beat around the bush.*
  - *When it feels right, say something like, "As you get to know me, does anything resonate? Do you know of anybody I should know? If so, will you connect me?"*
  - *Also, be sure to ask, "Is there anything I can do for you?"*
- ***Treat everyone you meet with respect.*** *They are doing you a favor by sharing their time and resources. Be curious about their own career path and ask thoughtful questions.*
- ***Think about other ways to expand your network.*** *Find networking events in your city. Consider your passions and hobbies—are there networks or organizations you could get involved in? These are good places to build more relationships.*
- ***If you plan to move to a new city, make it clear you have real plans.*** *People are wary of job applicants who say they'll move, but offer no specifics.*

**Mentality and Motivation Behind Networking**

It is tempting to want a formula for networking or connecting, but Gary's approach is more holistic and above all is *other-centric*, rather than self-centric. His story suggests a mentality and motivation behind networking that is more intent on relationship building than self-improvement. Here are points to consider as you reconstruct your own networking foundation:

- *Get outside yourself and ask how you can help others.* *It is natural to be self-consumed when networking. But instead of walking into a meeting thinking, "I hope this lands me a job," let your motivation be to help the other person. Not only does this make a better impression; it's a reminder to you that others have concerns beyond your goals.*
- *View your meetings as opportunities to build relationships.* *Networking activities are often transactional and seem to be a means to an end, but don't view them that way. What can you learn from those you meet?*
- *Your job does not define your worth.* *Remember this, and you will be less likely to feel intense pressure when meeting with people and figuring out what is next.*
- *Humility is key.* *Despite the positions and roles you've had, right now you need help from others. This is a good place to be, though it may not feel that way.*
- *Express gratitude.* *If someone goes out of their way to connect you to their contacts, be sure to extend your thanks. People are spending their time and energy to help you—look for opportunities to pay it forward.*
- *Believe that you will add value to another organization.* *Be confident in what you have to offer, including your non-expertise areas.*
- *Get out there and stay open to where your connections lead.*
- *Enjoy yourself!* *Enjoy the interesting people you meet and new opportunities to connect. There will be positive surprises along the way—watch for them and enjoy!*

Another executive, Frank, found networking to be key in setting up his Next Season.

*I spent the last five or six years of my career thinking about what I wanted to do next. My company hired a lot of consultants, and I thought that might be something I would like to do. After working for one company for so long, I wanted to see what else was out there. My advice:*

- *Use your connections to help you find something for after retirement. Networking and marketing yourself will take a lot of time, but it will pay off in the end. When possible, begin your intentional networking while still working.*
- *Use skills you already have. You can use the talents you utilized in your corporate job in a different environment after retirement.*
- *Spend a lot of time thinking and preparing, so retirement is in the back of your mind for a number of years before you actually transition. You can't begin thinking about retirement the day you're packing up your office.*
- *Do a self-assessment of your skills so you can really see your best place and decide ahead of time how productive you want to be.*
- *Don't try to do the transition alone. Talk to others. Get advice from your family, your spouse/partner, your friends, or even others in the business field. Sometimes they can see things about you that you can't.*
- *Broaden your interests and balance your life. You need to leave time for your family, work, hobbies, spiritual life, health, and time to just have fun.*
- *Take time off between your work and next job. But not too much. It can be seductive to do nothing, but you will end up stale and sluggish.*
- *Technology lets you work from anywhere. You can work from vacation and no one minds as long as you get the job done. I take calls looking at the ocean.*

There are natural ways to network while you work. It doesn't necessarily have to be laborious, but can involve your already-made connections and interests. Some strategies for networking/ exploring new opportunities include:

- Join alumni networks/chapters of your alma mater or advisory groups
- Continue membership with associations in your industry or area of interest
- Explore local groups who gather around an interest area that you have through community, Chamber of Commerce, YMCA, or place of worship
- Take up a cause which has a natural community of interest
- Explore online groups for any area of interest and read blogs/ articles
- Join online chat groups and groups on LinkedIn

Laura, a former Fortune 30 EVP, found it important to create a new community for herself, and give herself permission to do things she never had time to do. Laura offers her insights:

*In the years before I retired, I spent a ridiculous amount of time traveling. I was flying across the country multiple times a month, and got to feeling like I didn't even participate in my own life. I felt like I had groomed my direct reports well and had been success-ful, so I knew it was my time to transition. I wanted to focus on the things I had not had time for and I wanted to use my skills to give back to the community. My advice:*

- ***Transitioning can be a bittersweet pill.*** *It was a great relief to be with my family, but I didn't realize how structured my life was as an executive until that structure was gone.*
- ***Release the pressure.*** *I put a lot of unnecessary guilt on myself for doing ordinary things once I retired. I got upset when people made the assumption that I slept in, because I didn't want to seem like a slacker. That pressure dissipates over time though, so try to relax and enjoy this new season.*

- **Create a community for yourself.** *That comes automatically during your career, but you need to replace that community with new connections in the new parts of your life.*
- **Your planner doesn't have to be full.** *I created a parallel world for myself after my transition, where every minute was spent with tasks I'd created, like reading a crazy number of newspapers. Not every second has to be planned, though. Enjoy the flexibility.*
- **Try a little of everything.** *I have done some consulting work, served with not-for-profits, and sat on a for-profit board. Check it out and see what fits your new life best.*
- **Being an empty nester brings great opportunities.** *I travel with my husband now and we call it "dating with money."*
- **Maximize your time, even if you're just relaxing.** *This is the best part about being retired. When you are an executive, every second is full, but a lot of time is tied up in red tape that makes life tedious. Being retired, I can get things done efficiently and use my time in ways that make me happy.*
- **Accept that there will be difficult days.** *Even in the best transitions, you have to go through a grieving process when you leave a chunk of your life behind. Just know that it will get better.*
- **Don't let your ego get the best of you.** *During your career, your ego is constantly fed and you may compare yourself to your colleagues. I had to learn to gauge my success based on myself instead of based on the outside world.*

Nearly all the executives we interviewed underscored the importance of networking while they were still in their roles (ideally), and most certainly afterward. Doing so set them up better (or less well, if not done) for Next Season opportunities. They surprised themselves with the extensiveness of their networks and the enjoyment they found reconnecting with people and making new professional acquaintances.

## 6

# Your Plan

*100% structure, and 100% flexibility*

M OST EXECUTIVES have created dozens of plans throughout their careers: strategic plans, implementation plans, growth plans. Plans to divest, plans to acquire. And the strength of each plan, when reviewed 6 or 12 months later, was whether it held up through the test of time and whether it followed relatively unchanged from its original design.

Your new "transition plan" (which we will now refer to as *Your Plan*) does not share many characteristics with the other plans you spent your career developing, evaluating, and implementing. In fact, a great transition plan is one that evolves with time and learnings, and rarely stays the same when evaluated 6 or 12 months later.

We encourage you to adopt *100% structure, and 100% flexibility*. It is important to have a structured, specific plan. But it is equally important, if not more so, to be flexible and evolve that plan, or even change it completely as post-transition events and relationships unfold. You need to have options and the ability to adapt to whatever comes your way.

In fact, we encourage the use of "modifiers" when you answer the many questions about what you will do next. Our favorites are: "For now, . . . " or "Right now, . . . " which train you and your contacts that your Next Season will be defined by *changing characteristics* versus a single title/role or affiliation . . . and that change/transitioning is part of *Your Plan*.

One colleague, Jim, was a former Executive Vice Chairman and CFO of an international corporation. He felt intensely about the importance of planning:

........................................................................................................

*My company had a mandatory retirement age, so I knew when I'd be retiring years ahead of the actual date. I thought a lot about what I wanted to do, but ultimately the "where" trumped the "what." My wife and I wanted to move across the country to a warmer climate, and so I decided not to look for new responsibilities until we found a new home. Eventually I got both. My advice:*

- *Plan! You plan for every other phase of life, so make sure you also plan for this new phase—especially the non-financial aspects. Start with something basic like where you'd like to live or whether you want to work full time, part time, and/or give back to a not-for-profit. Making those initial decisions helps make settling on the specifics much easier.*
- *There are multiple phases of retirement. After moving and settling in, I began working for a private equity firm and traveling a lot for work. But after a few years I transitioned into a more leisurely lifestyle.*
- *Help the organizations that helped you. My college years were extremely formative for me, so I decided to give back to the school by serving on some of their committees and helping to fundraise.*
- *Use your free time to travel. If you can afford to, travel with your entire family. We've thoroughly enjoyed spending time away with our kids and grandkids. You'll make memories that will last a lifetime.*

- **Stay active.** *Be disciplined about engaging in things that interest you and learning new things.*
- **Take advantage of the control you now have.** *The best part of being retired is channeling your skills and abilities in whatever direction you want. You get to manage your schedule. You get to decide what you do and when.*
- **Make two lists.** *Name one Productive Things I Want to Do, the other Fun Things I Want to Do. You'll be surprised by how many overlap.*

Planning begins with a closer examination of you. What brings you joy? What would you hope never to have to do *ever* again? What have you wanted to do, but never had time for? What concerns do you have that, with time and effort, could be mitigated (e.g., your health/wellness, relationships with people, a nonprofit cause you care a lot about, your finances)?

If you were standing at the last day of your life, gazing back upon your lifetime, what would you hope to have accomplished? Where do you want to make/leave your impact on the world?

The answers to these questions begin to formulate your plan for transition and your first Next Season.

One former Chief Human Resources Officer for an international corporation, who prided himself on careful career planning, was caught off-guard without a plan for his retirement transition. He offers this advice:

*I spent my entire career having a game plan. I was deliberate in strategizing each move, never leaving anything to chance. I always knew what needed to be done. For some strange reason, however, I didn't have a plan for how I would spend my time during retirement. I thought it would be a natural transition: "I'm passionate about everything, so I'll find other things." Well, retirement came and there was no soft landing. My advice:*

- **Plan your retirement.** *Process this upcoming season before it arrives. Don't wait until you are already retired to figure it out. There are emotional ramifications that come without a plan!*

- ***Engage in mentally challenging/stimulating activities.*** *Know what you need. You've been living in a challenging landscape for most of your life, and to lose this altogether can be extremely disheartening.*
- ***Set realistic goals before retirement.*** *If you're thinking you'll start an abundance of new hobbies/activities post-retirement, think again. If you are not already incorporating such interests into your life now, you probably won't in retirement.*
- ***Schedule time to see people regularly.*** *Be intentional about extending invitations to people with whom you would like to be connected.*
- ***Spend your new time with those you love.*** *I have gotten to spend more time with my grandchildren and it has been wonderful.*
- ***Anticipate the changes ahead***—*physically, emotionally, and mentally. Give yourself space and time to adjust to this new lifestyle and to feel the normal ups and the downs of transition. Be gracious with yourself—you've earned it!*

We agree with Jim: have a game plan for retirement. For a successful transition, we have found it extremely important that executives have a plan . . . for day 1, for week 1, for year 1.

While you don't want to overschedule yourself, or perpetuate an unhealthy schedule of overcommitment, it is important to have things on the calendar day 1, week 1, year 1. And remember, just because you have a plan, doesn't mean it is set in stone.

Kathy, a former Fortune 20 EVP, offered the following reflection and advice about transition planning:

*My transition was wonderfully smooth because I spent a lot of time planning ahead. After 30 years of traveling for business, I was ready for a change in lifestyle. I gave my company 10 months' notice so that I could finish well and have time to plan my Next Season. My advice:*

- **Create a departure plan.** *Spend your final six months on the job preparing to leave so you can end well. Have a plan for the nine months following your transition so you can start well and have some structure in place.*
- **Create a written plan** *for things you want to do during retirement. This is sort of a bucket list for this chapter of your life.*
- **Define a purpose for your Next Season.** *Going in, I knew I wanted to spend more time with my family, spend time volunteering, and spend time going back to school to learn some things I had always wanted to learn.*
- **Take advantage of where you live.** *Explore your city and neighborhood.*
- **If you traveled a lot for business, plan a few vacations** *so you can cure your restlessness and experience travel in a whole new way.*
- **Flexibility is the best part.** *I've gotten to spend more time with my family and have a lot more time for self-reflection and doing things I have long wanted to do, but never had the time.*
- **Sample things before you commit.** *I tried out a number of volunteer opportunities before picking a few I wanted to stick with.*
- **Ask others for advice.** *Whether it be a transition advisor or a friend who has traveled this road before you, they can be helpful. Be open to their willingness to help.*
- **Adjust the elements of your life to fit your new structure.** *I rearranged my closet and office to fit my new role as a student and volunteer versus an executive.*
- **Be willing to try new things.**
- **Don't shortcut the planning.** *It's the most important part.*

At the end of the day, the skills you acquire through your job and career are those you take with you wherever you go. Wherever you can use those skills as a true asset is where you can deploy your time and talents. Some have likened their next phase of life as a *project* they are passionate about . . . something that can be planned ahead, executed at whatever desired pace, with whomever they choose, and with the ability to make changes and adjust at any time.

Never wake up asking yourself what you are going to do. Rather, wake up *excited for the things you plan to do*—even if it's just reading three newspapers, walking with a friend, taking your pet to the vet, or meeting friends for drinks and dinner.

Sometimes it takes a physical move to a different dwelling or new city to prompt/encourage new patterns of behavior. Many of our clients have tried long-term (temporary) rentals in new communities where they have closer access to things they love, plus opportunities to meet more people in their same phase of life. Others report that building a new home as a family project was engaging and bonding at the beginning of their Next Season, as it gave them a project to work on together and a shared investment in their future.

One executive confided about his learnings regarding the danger of moving too far outside of your skill set. He was intrigued with the idea of becoming a commercial arbitrator and was encouraged by some influential legal friends in the field who had observed his ability to negotiate remedies from legal actions. He worked hard in the years prior to his retirement to establish contacts in this new field and was encouraged that it would work out.

But in the end, he concluded that his skill set was not distinctive enough to compete with the many judges already operating in that space. In the process, though, he discovered that advisory work drew on his experience in a different working context and would give him the best of both worlds—a fresh perspective leveraging the experience he had gained over his career. And so, he pursued a Next Season in advising, and left the world of commercial arbitration to others. *Don't miss that this executive would not have gotten to this place had he not explored new interests or gone down this path.*

There are no should's or right answers when it comes to Your Plan, only that you create a plan to guide you and your priorities in the early days—especially until you figure out what you truly want to do in your first Next Season.

## The Consistent Top Three

In our interviews with executives post-transition, there was strong consistency among the top three priorities in Next Season *Plans*:

1. ***Spending time with family was quoted most often.*** Nearly every executive prioritized closing the gap between *time spent* with family and *value placed* on family. An interesting observation: in a world of two-career families, grandparents who lived close by seized the opportunity to be an integral part of their grandchildren's lives, since with two parents working there are many activities which the parents cannot attend. Many interviewees put a financial priority on paying for the family to travel to be together. They wanted the family to be together and to demonstrate that priority by enabling it to happen for their younger children/families.

2. ***Becoming more physically active was second most quoted.*** There was recognition by all executives of the importance of living a healthier lifestyle and a desire to make this a high priority when deciding how to allocate time and energy. Related: obtaining the best medical advice was also mentioned by several as a key concern for the future.

3. ***Spending time giving back/doing something that brings you deeper meaning and purpose was third.*** For some, this included engaging in not-for-profit work, teaching, or coaching. Others spoke of wanting to use their domain-specific skills to help where needed, either individuals or organizations. Executives reported early experiences with not-for-profit engagement—which led to important choices. All recognized that such work is important and worthwhile.

   Perhaps of greater importance was realization that the organizational skills of corporate executives are badly needed in the not-for-profit world. However, many expressed frustration at the negatives in some not-for-profits—limited resources, poor management, inefficiencies—which led people to be selective in choosing a not-for-profit. They felt it highly important to choose organizations whose causes tugged at the heartstrings or for which they felt passion.

Vanessa, a former Fortune 100 CEO/Chairwoman, offers helpful insight into planning and transition:

........................................................................................................

*I had planned and pondered retirement for years before the date arrived. I wanted to be on boards and do consulting work— but first I needed time to relax and think. Staying positive and enjoying the fruits of my labor was really important because I had worked hard for years. Now was my chance to reflect on all of the good I'd been able to do for the company and individuals I worked with. I also wanted to slow down a bit from my frenetic pace and life. My advice:*

- *Take time. Time to reflect on your accomplishments and consider your options before jumping into new endeavors. Waiting a little while before committing to things can give you a fresh perspective. And new doors may open in the meantime.*
- *Seek a new way to utilize your talents.*
- *Take the opportunity to try new things. I am now serving on a university board and loving the experience. I love interacting with the students, mentoring young people, and being involved in shaping so many lives.*
- *Pick and choose what you want to do. The best part of this phase of my life is that I get to decide how to spend my time and with whom. I love having more time to spend with those who matter to me.*
- *Create a new structure for yourself. You are used to having a lot of structure in your life. Just leave time/capacity within that structure so you have more freedom to use as you choose.*
- *Get involved with projects that bring you energy. I love working with young people because it energizes me while helping to create a lasting legacy.*

- **Add value to whatever you do.** *Just like you always have. Don't just show up.*
- **Take all the worries off your plate.** *I wish I had sold my big house sooner, because I worried about it more than I needed to.*

A lot of "retirement" is keeping your energy up and staying positive. Get up! Get involved! Get going!

Eli, a former Fortune 100 VP, chose to retire because he wanted a change:

*I retired because I wanted something new and different. So I gave 10 months' notice and began my next chapter. For a few months, all I did was relax, but I also looked for new ways to use the skills and expertise gained during my career. So I transitioned into consulting, and then to business startups. I was a founding principal of a business accelerator that brings management talent and seed financing to emerging technologies. This was an exciting new way to use my skill set. Retiring doesn't mean you have to be done working. If you enjoy what you are doing, it isn't really working anyway. My advice:*

- **Leaving a corporate position can be a dramatic change.** *After living within a certain routine for years, transitioning to something new can be daunting. Mentally preparing can make everything easier.*
- **Make plans and have goals, but don't put on blinders.** *Move into your Next Season with some forethought, but be open to new experiences and opportunities that might not arrive until after your transition.*
- **Take the opportunity to volunteer.** *Since leaving my corporate position, I've had more time to serve at my church and on the board of a local museum, both of which have been rewarding.*
- **Do what you want, when you want.** *That's the best part about being retired. Don't paint yourself into a box with too many commitments right away.*

- *Meet interesting people and open new doors.* The world is full of them. Take advantage of both in your Next Season.
- *Write down your goals and review them.* This can help you stay on track. Having a concrete mission can help you avoid saying "yes" to things you will regret later.
- *Take time to think and relax before jumping into your Next Season.* When you retire, people want to know how you plan to spend your time, but don't be in a hurry to answer that question.

Companies provide a platform for talented executives to use their gifts and talents. They use, reuse, refine, stretch—and sometimes overuse—those muscles to the benefit of the company, its people, and its business. With a transition to your Next Season, those gifts and talents stay with you. Always. It's just the platform you leave behind. Part of your new plan is deciding who will be the next beneficiaries of those amazing talents, bruises, learnings, and gifts.

# 7

## Achieving Purpose

*Find purpose in all your actions and time*

PERHAPS THE MOST IMPORTANT CRITERION for a successful Next Season is feeling you found purpose in what you do and how you spend your time. You are greeted with a transition from *have to do,* to *want to do*—and with that comes immense freedom and choice in how you will spend your time.

As George Bernard Shaw observed—

*This is the true joy in life, the being used for a purpose recognized by yourself as a mighty one . . . the being a force of Nature instead of a feverish, selfish little clod of ailments and grievances complaining that the world will not devote itself to making you happy.*

As Shaw implies, the gift of this season is the time to choose how you spend your time, energy, and expertise. Many executives find their purpose through engaging in things that mean the most to them: family, giving back, charitable causes that touch their heart—or that they feel the world needs some muscle behind.

Few people ever take the time to really contemplate their purpose. Purpose is different from goal, although they are often used interchangeably. Understanding our purpose requires us to allocate generous time and space to considering . . . what are we meant to do in our lifetimes? Where are our gifts and capabilities best used in service to the greater world or others? What brings us joy that we can feel from the top of our head to the tips of our toes? When do we feel the most proud, the most contributory, the most fulfilled? These are the questions we intend to explore when we address the issue of "purpose."

A former Fortune 10 VP, Ben, had the opportunity to serve others through not-for-profit work in Japan when he was growing up. Working the majority of his career in corporate America, he always knew that when he retired, he wanted to find a way to give back. Having a plan in place made his Next Season something he looked forward to. Now he is using his engineering and project management skills to dramatically impact the lives of those less fortunate. His advice:

- *Look to your past to inspire your future. My transition was about returning to an area of work that I had been unable to engage in fulltime for years. Whether going back to school or resuming an old hobby, your Next Season can be a great time to revisit your past.*
- *Give back through not-for-profit work. There are so many people around the world who could benefit from your help. Find a way to lend a hand.*
- *Repurpose your old skills. I use the administrative and management skills I gained working for a corporation to more effectively lead a not-for-profit, even though those fields are very different.*
- *Assess your financial situation. Obviously this will be high on your list as you consider the options for your Next Season.*
- *Enjoy the time with your family. I have five children and a number of grandchildren that I want to spend time with, so I*

*make sure that my life isn't so hectic that it cuts away from my time with them.*

- *Plan and work toward your Next Season. Your Next Season will not just happen, just like your career didn't just happen. You have to work hard and plan for this new chapter in your life, just as you did your previous chapters.*
- *Figure out what you are passionate about. What will satisfy you as you move forward? Make the most of this exciting new time in your life.*

Ben has dedicated his Next Season to bringing electricity to remote communities in Africa. He is combining his faith, project management skills, and engineering expertise to change the lives of others. He has found true purpose in his Next Season.

Another executive, Wayne, retired as a Director of a Fortune 100 industrial company. He wanted to give back in his Next Season. Like Ben, he felt a calling to do that after a successful corporate career:

*I wanted to get involved with not-for-profits while I was working, but I traveled so much that I didn't have the time. After retiring, I got involved in a lot of efforts within my community, which is where I felt called. It meant a lot to me to give back in this way, and I found the activity and engagement with new people very enjoyable. My advice:*

- *Ground yourself outside of what you do at work. This way your identity is not tied solely to what you do for a living. Take pride in the many roles you play. You're a lot more than your former job title.*
- *Stay grounded when you are a CEO. When your corporate perks are taken away, you will still have things to keep you happy and motivated.*
- *Consider assisting your replacement as a consultant. This is a great way to ease out of corporate life.*
- *Manage everything with your spouse or partner. In many cases, they struggle just as much as you do and need help transitioning as well.*

- **Use your free time to leave a legacy to your children and grandchildren.** One thing I'm doing for them is writing a book about where I've come from and what I've done.
- **Enjoy your freedom.** You get to do your own planning. Stay busy, but save time to relax.
- **Find a younger doctor and financial planner**—younger than you. This way you will have them for the long run.
- **Be comfortable as the person you are.** At parties you are no longer an executive, but a grandfather and an active board member in your community.

Tom, a former physician, found fulfillment in singing with the choir and praise band at his church. He is grateful for more time to read without interruption. His advice:

- **The gifts of retirement are time and choice.** Now I have plenty of time and the ability to choose my own ways to fill it.
- **Don't retire without a plan.** Are you going to put in time on a board, at the church, at school, at a second job, traveling? Don't retire without a plan. Have a clear place to spend your time.
- **Enjoy new reading time.** I've really enjoyed reading more during this season of life. I have more time, and can spend hours with a book now, where before I could only read for brief snippets of time if at all.
- **Use your career skills in new ways.** Since I was a doctor, I now volunteer with Hospice, which has impacted so many people during such a difficult time during their life.
- **Grow in your faith.** If you are religious, use retirement as a time to grow. I've become a much stronger and more committed Christian during this phase of life.
- **Improve your health.** Spend time focusing on your physical health as well as your mental and spiritual health.

In our work with executives, four themes seem to pinpoint what they enjoy most about their Next Seasons:

1. Having control over their own time and how they spend it
2. The flexibility to respond to unexpected opportunities of interest
3. Spending time with family in meaningful and helpful ways
4. Giving back to causes they care about

By far, the most direct benefit of post-corporate life is having control over your time and your activities. Over and over, we have heard this as the most often-cited reluctance to over-commit in retirement.

In addition, people value having the capacity to respond to invitations, to explore interesting ideas and possibilities, and to engage in something of interest. Having capacity and availability in their schedule was something highly unfamiliar to most executives.

Norman, a former Fortune 100 operating company president, found himself in retirement transition due to health. Unfortunately, his health also nullified his long-planned Next Season of building homes for persons in need. He continued a discernment process as he sought purpose for his next phase of life, and found it: leading a not-for-profit focused on food security for the hungry.

Norm's insights inspire one to retain optimism—even if you face personal obstacles. They encourage us to maintain a relentless search for purpose in our Next Season.

........................................................................

*When I had major back surgery, I decided it was time to retire. I had wanted to help build homes for those in need, but the surgery prevented this. I found a new unexpected calling working for a not-for-profit. It helped me make my Next Season a productive one, as it allowed me to greatly contribute with the skills I had gained in the corporate world. It really consumed my days and nights—and how I spent my weekends. Through this effort, I felt like I was making a difference and giving back. My advice:*

- ***Don't just sit around.*** *Initially I followed the stock market on television and bought groceries. Then I began to open my eyes to really ask myself, "What will my Next Season be? What do I want to do?"*

- **Seek activity.** *Being at home without a plan is not a sustainable way to spend retirement. You need to seek more activity.*
- **Apply the skills you learned in your years of business to new situations.**
- **Business people can really help not-for-profits.** *Look for those that need your specific skill set and whose mission is an interest area or passion for you.*
- **Spend more time with your loved ones.** *Retirement is a great time to make memories for your children and grandchildren.*
- **Plan activities for yourself.** *Family is important, but everyone has their own individual schedules and lives. People think family, golf, and travel, but a lot of time you need something more to fill up your days and give you purpose.*
- **A well-thought-out retirement plan is paramount.** *If you think you have it all figured out just by having a date to retire, you've already lost the battle. Put a lot of thought into the level of activity you want in your Next Season and where you specifically want to be involved.*
- **Never underestimate your ability to make a difference** *for and with people and populations who really need help.*

Regarding spending more time with family, co-author Bill offers an interesting insight similar to Norm's:

*It is not just about spending time with children and family, but also about figuring out how best to be helpful. Children of retirees are often young adults with their own priorities and challenges. We have found that we need to be sensitive to the impact we are having on their sense of independence. In some cases, like ours, it is exaggerated by the fact that we have not lived in the same area for many years.*

Toby, a former physician and Professor of Medicine, realized it was critical that she let go of her former way of living and give herself time to discover her Next Season purpose . . .

For years I'd let my work consume a large portion of my life. I worked long hours in the hospital and didn't trust others to handle my responsibilities while I was away. I couldn't even relax on vacations. It took me a little while to allow myself to relax in retirement, but since I have, I have found my Next Season to be a rewarding and healthier one. My advice:

- **Fear of flying.** Don't continue to work just because you fear what lies on the other side. At a certain point, fear of retiring may keep you from making the choice that's better for your family, your health, and your mind.
- **Apprehension and separation anxiety**—that's what I felt when I started to think about retirement. This is natural, but it's important to push through the apprehension thoughtfully, to plan your transition, and to understand you are making the right decision. I suffered some guilt for not being at work for the first few months, but the transition was easier than I expected. You just have to keep moving forward.
- **Keep learning.** I've been a lifelong learner. I've loved learning about patients and diseases, and I didn't want to stop learning. So I've been taking classes at seminary and reading to stay sharp.
- **Don't let your health go.** When I retired I had a bad knee, but instead of sitting around and letting the knee grow worse, I've taken up an exercise rehab regimen that involves a lot of walking, swimming, and water aerobics. Now my knee is much better and I haven't lost my mobility.
- **Plan ahead.** If you are a type-A who is worried about feeling unfulfilled, then plan ahead so you have things to do when you retire. Just make sure they are things you want to do and not just have to do.
- **Music is a wonderful thing to rediscover in retirement.** I'm taking piano lessons and a lot of my friends are picking up their old instruments as well.

- *I laugh, smile, and sing more.* This season of life has been happy, healthy, and purposeful for me. Sometimes you don't realize how wonderful relaxing is until you give yourself time to do it.

A blog written by our colleague Deborah Dellinger provides an insightful perspective on how executives spend their time after they conclude their season of corporate leadership.

VIEWPOINT

## How Will You Spend Your Time Post-Transition?

*Deborah Dellinger, Director of External Engagement*
*My Next Season*

WHO RECEIVES THE BENEFIT *of your hard-earned skills and experience in your first season after retirement?* Everyone has an opinion, offering strong, valid reasons to turn your focus toward their agenda as you transition from productivity to purpose. But it's your choice, not theirs. Using your executive skills for a larger purpose offers unique opportunities to give back as well as significant physical and mental health benefits.

*Volunteering can bring a sense of identity and purpose as part of your transition—and it can lead to a longer, healthier life.* Two studies using data from the *Americans' Changing Lives Survey* (Institute for Social Research, University of Michigan) found that volunteering increases life satisfaction, feelings of good health, happiness, and positive self-esteem, and reduces depression. In two other studies, participants reported that volunteering improved their mental health.

*The key is to discern what roles or activities are meaningful to you.* One study notes that each role "amplifies opportunities to increase social networks, power, prestige, resources, and emotional gratification"—which reduces depression symptoms. Volunteers often find purpose and fulfillment in their work with charitable organizations and discover that the work really matters. A Japanese study found decreased depression in volunteers when compared to non-volunteers.

*By focusing on purpose, community, relationships, and developing a plan, you enjoy the benefits of continued positive social networks and roles.* Among people who are diagnosed with a medical condition, those who volunteer cope better, which positively affects the severity of their condition and their prognosis. Volunteering strengthens social networks and reinforces roles, positively impacting health outcomes.

Researchers studying this dynamic found that cancer and heart disease victims who also have strong social networks achieved better outcomes than those who do not. People who volunteer have less depression, slower decline in functioning, and lower mortality compared with those who do not volunteer.

Likewise, volunteering to use your leadership and domain-specific skills (such as coordinating, envisioning, and managing people and processes) staves off cognitive decline. Physical exertion associated with volunteering also enhances cognitive functioning.

*So, what roles will you play in your Next Season? How will you spend your time?*

The good news is: you decide what "purpose" looks/feels like to you. It only matters that your gifts and talents have been engaged to your satisfaction and that how you spend your time aligns with your values.

One of our clients, Martha, offers the following perspective, and speaks to her finding purpose after transitioning from her role as a Fortune 50 senior executive. Her advice:

- ***Repurpose your skills.*** *Think about the skills you have developed over your career and how you might be able to use them in a new way. I was able to transfer my skills in finance, strategic planning, due diligence, and mentoring into a new role as officer and board member of one of the largest U.S. not-for-profits. The change is exciting and I feel I am living into my purpose. It is also fulfilling to use the skills I spent years developing.*
- ***Plan both your exit and your Next Season entrance.*** *Before I retired, I agreed to deepen my service on a couple of non-profit boards. After I retired, I extended my volunteer work through my church and into education, both areas where I have tremendous passion. I consciously booked my time early on, doing things that were meaningful to me.*
- ***Your new-found free time is not endless.*** *It will be quickly absorbed by people and organizations who want to tap into your talents. Decide how you want to spend your time—and be comfortable saying "no" to things that fall outside what you see as your purpose.*
- ***Resist temptation to continue your same work.*** *Even if you think you want to continue to work, resist the temptation (or calls from search firms) to immediately jump back into doing the same thing at a different firm or something new. Take some time to really understand what you want your Next Season to look like.*
- ***Strengthen and renew your friendships.*** *Now that you have more time, develop your bonds with others. I rarely had the time to take a leisurely lunch or a long walk in the neighborhood with a good friend. It is a true gift now that I try to embrace as much as possible.*

It is hard to know when you have "achieved purpose." It is not a black-and-white concept, and it looks different at different stages of life. As we have suggested throughout this book, life post-career seems to mirror life in a broader context: seasons defined by different characteristics, which flow one into the other. It may be that one's purpose evolves and changes with time, or that you live more deeply into it with time.

We found ourselves most inspired by the many, many, many executives with whom we spoke, who saw their Next Season as an invitation to live more fully into their purpose.

# 8

## More Changing Seasons

*Above all, have grace in your transitions*

ONE THING IS CERTAIN: THERE WILL ALWAYS BE CHANGE. And as we grow older, more variables come into play in our lives, impacting how we feel and spend our time. Many executives begin to relive aspects of their earlier years as the needs of grown children and/or aging parents become a major factor in daily life. Even if it is not through direct delivery of care or face-to-face contact, concerns for support and remaining physically proximate become material influencers of decisions, such as where to live and where time must be spent.

Some seasons are out of our control, whereas others can be predicted and managed. Co-author Bill makes this observation:

*My wife and I are now in our third Next Season. Our experience reveals several themes that are reasonably predictable and which are best anticipated:*

1. *Desire/ability for long-distance travel*
2. *Presence of grandchildren*

3. *Currency of career networks and experience*
4. *Desire to be part of local communities*

*These can drive significant decisions. In our case, looking back over our three Next Seasons, each was driven by a specific need—*

> *Season One: Escaping from corporate life.*
> *Season Two: Reestablishing our Canadian roots.*
> *Season Three: Becoming participants in our son's family and grandson's lives.*

*Each Next Season has had its own rhythm; each has brought its own gifts.*

VIEWPOINT

## Personal Reflections on My Changing Seasons

*Bill Innes, Co-Author of* Your Next Season

WE STARTED OUR PLANS for our Next Season One a couple of years before I retired. The centerpiece was a new home on a remote and very beautiful beach on Grand Cayman. Judy and I had a lot of fun planning all the details, even building a model ourselves. I mention this because *the act of planning and building the model* created for us a reality about our new life.

In my case, it was doubly important because I was unable to retire as soon I had expected, and planning kept us engaged in our future. The time also enabled me to start making contacts for my Next Season's purpose: to get into industrial arbitration.

Next Season One was all we had expected, but it also came with its share of the unexpected—our house was destroyed by a hurricane before we could occupy it (thank goodness my retirement was delayed), and industrial arbitration turned out to be a bust. But the house and location provided the complete break from the corporate world that I needed, and I discovered the world of leadership consulting, now with over two dozen fascinating clients!

Next Season Two was about returning to our roots. We had lived all over the world, which was fascinating and rewarding, but along the way we seemed to have lost something important about ourselves. We are fortunate to have our roots in a large family and a wonderful country. We felt that it was time to reconnect, and to give back.

So, in Next Season Two, we traded our house for a condo in Cayman, which we could more easily visit for part of the year, and established a new base in eastern Canada. We also discovered, like many others, that moving home is not as easy as you might think. It took a lot of work to make and reestablish the network of business and family relationships.

It is a humbling fact that you may have had a big job on a global scale, but it doesn't give you automatic access to the more closed world of people who have worked together for their whole lives. It's also frustrating yet again to be a new member at the golf club—no matter how well you play! (which was not an advantage I could rely on!)

In Next Season Two, it was again helpful that we had anticipated our Next Season—we bought a condo and joined the golf club well in advance, and engaged the family in anticipating our return. I was greatly helped by old friends who encouraged me to join a couple of think tanks where my international experience was really valued.

Next Season Three was marked by arrival of our grandson, and we, like many others, were surprised by the marked change in our priorities—to be a more integral part of our immediate family. In parallel, my interests shifted toward legacy issues—a collaboration with my brother on our family history and building a national discussion about what is distinctive about being Canadian.

We also made the decision, now in our early seventies, to build our dream home on 17 acres looking out over the Gulf islands off the coast of British Columbia. Many of our friends think we are nuts! But we are exercising again those muscles of making a new life, actually participating in the life of our grandson, and having the fun of building the house we have dreamed of for 50 years! Not all plain sailing as you might imagine, but full of challenges we can actually solve, which is great therapy in view of the world we live in.

One final and important word: one constant throughout our Next Seasons has been that I have been privileged to be able to continue to advise fascinating clients about interesting business issues—the technology may change, but the essentials remain the same.

Just as we transition from winter to spring, we know that summer and fall will come, too. The circle of life ensures this, whether we want it or not—and with it come transitions in our own lives, too. It is important, above all things, to have grace in these transitions. Grace first and foremost toward yourself as you go through changes physically, emotionally, spiritually, intellectually, and to others around you.

Patricia, a former Fortune 20 Managing Director, offers her thoughts precisely on this point:

*I've really lived through two retirements at this point. When I initially transitioned out of my corporate role, I wanted to keep working but in a different setting, so I took a position as a university administrator. Now a few years later, I'm moving out of fulltime work and discovering a Next Season for the second time. Retirement isn't a "one-and-done" experience, but a series of exciting choices and transitions. My advice:*

- ***Accept when it's time to move on.*** *I could feel myself losing intensity toward the end of my corporate career, and I knew I needed a slower pace of life. I could have hung on a few more years, but I did what was best for me at the time.*
- ***Consider self-assessment.*** *I talked with my friends and former colleagues and attended an intensive executive program designed to assist in career transitions. This helped me focus in on what I really enjoy doing as well as what I am good at.*
- ***Consider working at a university.*** *It can offer a balance between the corporate world and a not-for-profit. A university is often run more like a business in that there is more structure, but it also has the not-for-profit mentality where the focus isn't as concentrated on efficiency and the bottom line.*
- ***Have realistic expectations at a not-for-profit.*** *Your experience as a top-tier executive will be valued, but you will need to be sensitive to the organization's employees, policies, and experience. Don't expect to make changes on the first day; there will be a lot for you to learn as well. Listen before making decisions.*
- ***A not-for-profit can be both rewarding and frustrating.*** *It may not be as stressful as a corporate job, but resources are limited and the pace of decision-making can be slow.*
- ***Do something that excites you when you wake up daily.*** *This is a season of life where you have more flexibility, so do things that make you happy.*
- ***Have days with nothing scheduled.*** *With this free time, I've visited museums, gone to the movies, met up with friends, or just stayed in to read a book. Don't worry about boredom: you can counter that if and when it comes.*
- ***Change your plan if it's not working.*** *I know I have a hard time quitting something once I start, but at this point in life, I think it is more important to enjoy what you are doing. Make the most out of this Next Season in your life and every experience you choose to create.*

In our first Next Season, part of what happens is learning how to transition well, including acceptance of your new self and others. Once you are through the biggest transition—moving on from your structured corporate life—each subsequent transition becomes much easier.

Joe, a former international SVP, thought of his career in terms of seasons:

*I've always set goals for myself: physical, mental, and career. When I accomplished everything I wanted to in my career, I decided it was time to retire and focus on other aspects of my life. In this Next Season, I have goals as well, and because of these I don't feel unproductive. I'm still working toward something. My advice:*

- ***This season of life is a great time to see the world.*** *Traveling for longer than a couple of days is now possible, and my wife and I take advantage of the opportunity, sometimes for weeks on end.*
- ***After I retired, I continued to teach as an adjunct college professor.*** *Teaching can be a great way to add structure to your life and make some extra money without having the time constraints of a regular job.*
- ***Take up old hobbies.*** *I used to fish when I was younger, but hadn't picked up a rod in years. I took a refresher course at a local college and have loved getting back on the water.*
- ***Do what you love.*** *I love golf and now I play more than the occasional game. I practice at the driving range, play with friends, and have even traveled around the world to play some of the more prestigious courses.*
- ***Think outside the box and try something new.*** *I've always been fascinated by bridges, so I took an art class to learn to draw them. Now I'm planning to write a kids' book about bridges.*
- ***Write down your goals to make them more tangible.*** *Try making lists like "50 Things I Want to Do in the Next 10 Years."*

- **Stay active to keep in good health.** *I go on daily walks with my wife, but I also do yard work, go get the groceries, work out, and play golf. Exercise doesn't have to be dreaded.*
- **My time is mine.** *When I was working, even Saturdays were not free. Now I'm like a 10-year-old on summer vacation! The time is mine, and I get to decide how I spend it, which has been a wonderful gift.*

The metaphor we are using, of life's changing seasons, is thoughtfully chosen. Your first big transition out of corporate life is much like the transition from winter to spring. Spring is full of color and possibility.

Bulbs planted last fall and in the autumns before, long forgotten, come up. Others, though nurtured and cared for meticulously, may not be as marvelous as you had expected. Hard rains and dark days lie behind the vibrant intensity of springtime colors and flowering.

Other flowers appear in strange places, where the wind and birds dropped seeds you never knew about. These random flowers often take root on their own, and are stunning among your otherwise carefully tended garden. And while the result may be different from what you envisioned, the truth is it is even more beautiful.

Unexpected beauty abounds in your spring season, including the gift of the bare spots that persist despite your planting, as they enable the full radiance of the flowers to shine through.

Jim, a former technology Chairman, President, and CEO, offers this perspective:

*You can have your cake and eat it too. I've started my own company, serve on boards, work with not-for-profits, and serve at my church. In this season, you don't have to limit yourself to just one thing. My advice:*

- **Work with people you like.** *Whether it be a for-profit organization or your alma mater, make sure you are with people with whom you want to work and enjoy.*

- *Be clinical in understanding what you enjoy and why.* *Sometimes an assessment test can help you define your skills in a new light. One season, thankfully, leads to another where you may do different things.*
- *Talk to as many people as you can.* *Sometimes others can understand what you need better than you do.*
- *Find a hobby you love* *but haven't spent time with in a while. I enjoy landscape photography, but had little time for it at the height of my career. I fully anticipate that in several years, I may be engaged in something different.*

With each season comes the expected and unexpected; some things are more than we hoped, and others we anticipated as being so important turn out to be non-factors.

Vivaldi captured it stunningly in his famous Four Seasons concertos, where the musical intensity varies from fast, to slow, to fast again as you navigate through four seasons of music (in 12 concertos). It is our own story as well; fast, slow, fast again—and eventually slow and slower.

The career of Mark, a retired U.S. Air force Brigadier General, mirrored Vivaldi's Four Seasons: dramatic, intense movements, punctuated by incredible crescendos and decrescendos. Mark shared the following:

*After spending over 30 years in the aerospace industry, I wanted to have some different experiences. I went from the Air Force to taking a year off, to being President of a public company, to owning a Chick-fil-A. My mantra was "I'm not making a decision for the rest of my life. I'm just making a decision for what I'd like to do next." I decided that I would try something for three years, and if I didn't like it, I would try something else. I have no regrets. Instead, I have stories that I hope will help others. My advice:*

- *Think about what you really want to do.* *Give yourself time to process the transition, both intellectually and emotionally.*

- **Don't rush into anything.** *This is a significant life transition. Take time to assess what has made you feel fulfilled in the past, what you do well, and where there is a need. It can fit together like a puzzle.*
- **Balance contemplation with action.** *You'll know when you are ready. Don't overthink or wait for the perfect opportunity. Remember that you are not making a life-long decision. If you are interested in something, try it for a while. If you don't enjoy it, try something else.*
- **Get out of your normal routine.** *Open your mind to new possibilities.*
- **YOU have to make it happen.** *No one is going to figure out this next stage for you.*
- **Think about how you can give back.** *Everyone has something different to contribute and offer.*
- **Don't just drift into something.** *Once you make a decision and head in a direction, opportunities will present themselves.*
- **Enjoy the flexibility.** *Time is your asset.*

It is important to remember that there is not just one Next Season—but many more changing seasons. Grace and acceptance are key. Some transitions we initiate, whereas others happen whether we will them to or not. And thank goodness for that!

# 9

## Your Spouse/Partner Has a Next Season Too

*Talk and plan your hopes and dreams together*

W HAT IS OFTEN NOT REALIZED by the executive preparing to transition, is that spouses and partners—especially those who have foregone their own careers to be the at-home parent-in-charge—experience stressors of the same magnitude.

Your spouse or partner—who has dedicated their own life at home while you pursued your career, who actively parented the children, who has been your trusted advisor through corporate lifecycles and leadership challenges—also goes through a huge career transition when the last child leaves the nest and/or when you retire.

In fact, it is no less difficult for your companion to navigate this transition. The only difference is that there are no retirement parties, no formal honors nor recognition of contributions, no gifts nor plaques for the differences made for decades of selfless service.

Deciding what to do next is not easy for anyone who has enjoyed success in their main-stage career, whether in the workplace or the home space. Recognizing that this is a huge transition for *both* members of a couple is an important first step. Empathy and encouragement need to flow generously in both directions. It is essential that both parties be part of the Next Season planning. It is, after all, a Next Season for you both.

It is important at this stage, especially, to recognize the myriad other roles your spouse or partner has undertaken, separate from you. Most executive spouses have had to be strong, highly independent, and self-sufficient and have created their own active, productive, and fulfilling life.

A career transition impacts both parties individually and on their life together. The clarity of purpose, rules of the journey, and destination are all reset with this transition. For some, new fears emerge about how decisions will be made, what life will look like post-transition, how each of you will adjust and find new rhythms.

The single action found to be most universally helpful at this juncture is to *talk* about the transition. While conversing with one another, it is also useful to develop a plan and continually refine it. Identify your concerns, both of you. Identify your hopes and dreams. Discuss options.

Be open when things are working or not working. Keeping your lines of communication wide open is critical to the successful transition of you both. Several executives mentioned how helpful it was to have a joint project that they could work on together prior to the formal retirement (e.g., building a new or second home).

Rich, a former private company President and CEO, offers valuable insights on the importance of spouse partnership:

*After working for 17 years in public policy and moving to the corporate world for another 20, I'm now ready for what my wife and I call "Life 3.0." I'd been working with my board leadership* for five years on a strong succession plan, so I knew they were in good hands when it was time for me to leave. When most people think about what they want to do after retirement, they think of themselves as an individual. But for anyone who is married, these decisions are for both of you. It is very important that your spouse plays the role they want and deserve in your plans moving forward. My advice:

- **Do some research.** My wife and I talked to a dozen couples and read several books as we looked forward to our retirement. Many suggested that we "hit the pause button" and take a sabbatical to refocus. We're going to take three to six months off, do some traveling, and refocus on the things we want to pursue in "Life 3.0."
- **Embrace spontaneity.** As I was about to retire, I was asked to lead a year-long civic project that was very important to our region and our state, so we pushed back our sabbatical. It's been an enriching experience but required flexibility with respect to our initial plan.
- **Focus on your faith.** My wife and I find our faith very important. It drives our life, so we're using our new found time to engage more in faith-based causes, in prayer, and in studying scripture.
- **Leverage your strengths.** My wife and I have different strengths and weaknesses. As one team in this new phase of life, we can work off each other to be a more effective pair. I am called to be in a supportive role as she leads based on her strengths.
- **Don't be afraid to say no.** When you are approached with offers for things to do in your Next Season, many of them will be appealing and tempting. Don't be afraid to say no to things that don't fit with your schedule and priorities. Be discerning about your choices and recognize that you are seeking the "best yes."

## A PARTNER Framework

Like many things in life, we have found it helpful to have a structure for conversation about the future to ensure that the dreams and concerns of both of you are considered in the planning phase. We offer the acronym PARTNER as a framework to guide your conversations and early planning efforts. (A more detailed version of this framework to help guide your conversation together is in "Your Next Season Tools" at the back of the book.)

..........................................................................................

**P**riorities          *What priorities and goals do we have for this Next Season?*

**A**lternatives          *What alternatives do we have in how we spend our time?*

**R**ealities          *What current realities/constraints do we have to work within?*

**T**ogetherness          *What things do we want to achieve together?*

**N**on-togetherness    *What things do we wish to pursue independently?*

**E**vents and actions    *What are our actions/next steps?*

**R**evisiting our plan    *When will we revisit our plan to see how we are doing?*

..........................................................................................

The silver lining of your Next Season, beyond just hairlines, is that this is a time for each of you to pursue passions you have kept at bay while you have lived for your work. This timing presents opportunities for both of you to make a difference in things or people you care about through your presence and engagement in areas for which you lacked bandwidth before.

Whether through volunteering for a non-profit, mentoring others, being (more) present for neighbors, friends, and family members, or at last pursuing dreams and desires, this is a season of unlimited possibilities in a world with great needs. Remember, though, that it is a Next Season for Two—and for the two of you together. Spouses/partners need to be front and center in the Next Season contemplations and planning—from the very start.

# 10

## Lessons from Executives Post-Transition

*Eight major themes to consider*

THERE IS MUCH TO BE LEARNED from those who have walked before us and who pause to share their experiences and lessons learned. We have interspersed the insights of many executives throughout this book. After interviewing hundreds of executives post-transition, we gleaned eight major themes:

1. ***The quality of your transition and your Next Season is very much tied to how your previous season came to a close.*** This seems to be universally true. It is important to achieve closure on your work experience prior to its ending to enable the most positive transition to your Next Season.

2. ***The need to be thoughtful in advance about this next stage in life was universal.*** A year in advance seemed to meet most people's needs, although several executives with more elaborate transition plans saw a need for more

time. There is a real need for a comprehensive checklist of things to consider and real value in coaching from someone who has gone through the process several times. This ensures that important subjects are covered and executives work through the more difficult, unanticipated issues.

3. ***Those whose transition was abrupt or driven by factors outside their control were very dissatisfied in their Next Season and had trouble moving on.*** Note to corporations: consider being more explicit with executives as they enter senior positions in that the timing of their retirement likely will be driven by factors impacting the company, not by the executive's personal preference. Having this conversation explicitly could prompt some important contingency planning. All parties would benefit through building early discussion of transition and Next Season planning into occasions where topics like financial planning and retirement benefits are discussed.

4. ***Some executives' sense of self seems to be driven not only by their role, but also by their membership in the corporate community they are leaving.*** They are often unhappy about losing that affiliation, even though they have pursued substantive roles in retirement. Another note to corporations: consider encouraging executives to begin building other community affiliations long before they leave. Our interviewees suggest three years in advance. In addition, the many with whom we spoke who had continued some relationship/affiliation with their former employer in an advisory or other capacity found that continued connection incredibly reinforcing. They were pleased to be in a position to use their former employer's business card for several years.

5. ***Career extension versus new life stage.*** There was a sharp divide between those who viewed their next stage as an extension of their careers, with the attendant control-stature-recognition, and those who saw retirement as a new stage in their lives, driven by self-actualization and what they enjoyed.

- Several mentioned the need to really give thought to what you enjoy, because the easy default is to continue what you have always done and thus miss the opportunity to venture in a new direction—and this opportunity may not come again.

6. **The role of board work.** Many felt that board work was the logical extension of their executive role. "I really enjoyed being an enterprise leader, and board work seemed the closest thing to what I had enjoyed."

  - But many mentioned that board work was not a substitute for their corporate leadership role. The advisory nature of board work was a significant adjustment, and they really missed being at the center of decision-making. "Once you have run a company, being a director is not that much fun."
  - "Smaller companies are more interesting—because you are closer to the business strategy. Large company boards tend to be preoccupied with governance/liability issues."
  - Most seemed to think that three or four boards was about right, allowing room for personal time flexibility. As one person said, "It takes about 50% of my time, but the problem is that you don't control which 50%."
  - Several mentioned liability concerns and the importance of getting a very good understanding of the quality of the company and the board process—even to the extent of having them checked out by a law firm. Several mentioned that when a company gets in trouble, the board's time demands can be very onerous.
  - An often-cited suggestion was to get good advice from other board members about the quality of board opportunities.
  - For some, the due diligence/liability concerns of board work become more onerous and detract from satisfaction in the position. Several mentioned a significant increase in the number of calls and unscheduled meetings, which makes the planning of board work with other opportunities more challenging.

- It seems that most interviewees considered board involvement ahead of other vehicles for maintaining involvement with the corporate world—consulting, advisory work, etc.

7. ***Repatriation of expatriated executives at retirement is a particularly challenging situation.*** This deserves specific consideration by corporations:
   - Repatriation, although it occurs after retirement, is just as demanding on the family as expatriation was. It requires a similar level of corporate support with the additional complexities of taxation and estate planning issues.
   - Repatriating retirees face the dilemma of returning to their home country without a current network of contacts, which is so important in finding satisfying interests in their Next Season. Corporations can be very helpful in helping the executive find suitable opportunities.
   - Counseling of expatriated executives well in advance of retirement can be critical in helping them understand the demands of effective repatriation, and encourage them to start the process of building a bridge to their Next Season early.

8. ***Hitting the ground running when you retire.*** Several interviewees mentioned the importance of this—having things planned to do at the outset, even of a personal nature:
   - Make the move to your chosen location in advance, so that you are already started on building the social network you will need.
   - If possible, start some of the board or charitable associations while you are working, so they provide continuity through transition.
   - Have a project like building a home as a buildup to your new season.

## What Do Executives Miss Most Post-Transition?

*Responses to this question from our executive interviews:*

1. *Company affiliation and relationships.* They missed the sense of family/affiliation experienced through their work and the pride that came from being connected to the company/role/people.

2. *Leading people and the satisfaction of seeing them succeed.* Those for whom this was important sought coaching, counseling, and teaching in their Next Season as a way to scratch that itch.

3. *Being at the heart of complex decisions and feeling as though their work was making a great impact.* Those who desired this in their Next Season were more apt to seek a leadership position in a not-for-profit they cared about, or to take a leadership role in a smaller or personal endeavor.

4. *The quality of corporate colleague relationships.* They missed their colleagues and the comradery. There were many stories of executives whose friendships with former colleagues deepened after they left the company, no longer encumbered by organizational levels or issues. Several executives shared stories of how their former employers were intentional in treating retirees as "alumni" and planfully uniting and engaging them after leaving the company. Executives who were given such invitations universally accepted them and were grateful for the opportunity to stay connected with their past life in a small, but meaningful way.

The exit of key executives is a shared responsibility. The transition experience has a material impact, both on the executive and on the reputation of the corporation with an important constituency.

# 11

## Closing Thoughts

*Be choiceful in your Next Season*

THE TRANSITION TO YOUR NEXT SEASON starts from an unprecedented position of strength. You likely have the good fortune of being financially secure, with an established reputation, at the peak of your skills with a lifetime of experience, and many years of healthy life ahead of you. Others of you will go on to pursue income-earning opportunities that further extend and capitalize on your incredible gifts and talents.

Regardless of income-earning needs or lack thereof, it is important to seize the opportunity and be choiceful about what you do in your Next Season. Gone are the years of uncertainty and struggling to establish yourself, of building your resources, and making your mark. It is clearly a pivotal moment to embrace and cherish.

This book has been about how to make the most of this opportunity and to share the wisdom and insights of those who have made the transition to their Next Season. The situation of each executive is as varied as we are different as people, but there are a number of themes that seem to have universal value:

- ***This is your unique opportunity.*** It will define your next phase of life. You can think it through with the confidence that you will never be better prepared and less constrained. With all your career-building years behind you, it is your unique opportunity to think about what you really would ENJOY doing with your life going forward. You have paid your dues. Now it's time to explore and find what will give you personal joy and satisfaction.

- ***Your Next Season is just the first of many.*** Many executives find it useful to think of multiple seasons with various themes that drive their priorities—escaping the corporate world, reconnecting with their community, becoming part of their grandchildren's lives, pursuing a lifelong passion or interest. Themes like these can impact where and how you live and may require deeper, longer-range consideration.

- ***Start the transition before you retire.*** It is never easy to find the time in your busy executive schedule, but thinking this through with your spouse/partner is a great way to welcome this major transition into your lives as a shared endeavor. It will make the change much less stressful if it becomes a part of the continuum of your lives. In addition, many of the contacts/arrangements you will need to make may be unfamiliar and will take time to establish. It is really helpful if there is minimal "dead space" between your corporate life and the activities of your Next Season. If there is a lull, it may be a good time to take that trip of a lifetime—to sit back, enjoy what you have achieved, and celebrate your new freedom.

- ***Think about the balance between your commitments and unstructured time.*** This is particularly important regarding your family. In your Next Season, your unstructured time itself becomes an important commitment. Particularly with grandchildren—their needs, and your opportunity to be an intimate participant in their lives, is very often unscripted—and once lost, cannot be retrieved.

- *You are entering unknown territory.* The opportunities that you imagine at the outset often are overtaken by things you did not at all anticipate. A joy of this period in your life is having the flexibility to take on things you never thought of!
- *Pay attention to your health.* This is obvious, but it bears repeating: your health determines the quality of your Next Season more than any other factor. You now have the opportunity to dedicate time to regular exercise, so go for it—but don't be too ambitious. It is better to have a sensible program and stick to it.
- *Not investing in your health is cumulative.* This is insidious, sneaking up on you. There doesn't seem to be much difference in your sixties, but the difference in what you are able to do after age 70 becomes dramatic—and for an executive contemplating retirement in their early sixties that difference is huge.
- *Continue to learn.* A colleague who is approaching 90 and is still very active, with a wide circle of influence, advises that "the secret of a long and happy life is to remain invested in the future."
- *Stay open, remain relevant.* The increasing pace in the evolution of knowledge provides a fascinating opportunity to grasp ideas which have never been possible, and you need to do so to stay relevant.
- *Don't get trapped by administrative burden.* Now is the time to focus on things that exercise your mind and body, and nurture your soul. Keep it simple and engage assistance with the administrative duties.
- *Be a good partner—worth your weight in gold.* In many respects this is now your companion's time. After many years in which his or her priorities were secondary to the demands of your career, this is the time when you can share the opportunity of this Next Season together (there is a debt to be paid!).

Finally, we surveyed our executive clients about what if anything surprised them about the transition to their Next Season. We heard these common themes:

- **How well it had gone**—given the fear that many expressed at the outset.
- **How difficult the idea of retirement is after a lifelong career;** and how powerful it is to view it as an opportunity.
- **The need to become very good at self-initiation.** One of the realities of your Next Season is that if you don't do it, it likely won't get done!

We wish you well on your journey. Have faith. And recall . . .

*To everything there is a season,*
*and a time to every purpose under heaven.*

The following "**Your Next Season Tools**"
are excerpts from the MY NEXT SEASON
company's Workbook and advisory tools.
They are intended to help you begin thinking
about and preparing for your Next Season.

# Your Next Season Tools

## A. Personal Preferences Inventory

*Here are sample questions for your Personal Preferences Inventory, to be done during "The Pause" (Chapter 3).*

### Section 1—Parameters

1. **Geography**
   a. Do you have any commitments that constrain you geographically?
   b. What are your early thoughts about where you'd like to live all or some of the time?

2. **Financial**
   Are there financial concerns or considerations that impact how you want to spend your Next Season?

3. **Medical**
   a. Are there any personal or family medical concerns or constraints that impact your plans?
   b. Are there any personal objectives you have for yourself physically that will impact your time/priorities after your transition?

4. **Commitments You Bring with You**
   a. Are there any groups, organizations, or people to whom you feel a strong commitment that you see yourself needing to honor in this Next Season?
   b. Who might those be?
   c. Approximately how much time does fulfilling these require?

5. **Time**
   As you consider how you might spend time after you leave your current job, list things you have always imagined yourself possibly doing (for example, playing golf, speaking to audiences on favorite topics, reading three newspapers every morning, volunteering, reading novels, joining a gym, traveling, writing a book, taking classes, learning a language, working, spending time with grandchildren).

6. **Your Definition of Success**
   a. Sitting here today, describe what "success" looks like to you on the other side of this transition out of your organization.
   b. Describe any particular concerns you have about the transition.

7. **Caring for Others**
   Do you have obligations or caregiving responsibilities that impact how or where you will spend your Next Season?

# Section 2—The Highlights

*Please complete the following sentences.*

**1. I love**

**2. I am happiest when**

**3. The following things have been the highlights of:**
- My past year
- My past decade
- My most recent job
- My career
- My community life
- My marriage/partnership
- My children/grandchildren
- My friendships

**4. Work accomplishments I am the most proud of:**

**5. Non-work accomplishments I am the most proud of:**

**6. A good day for me is one in which (*check all that apply*):**

| | |
|---|---|
| ☐ I have a schedule for the day | ☐ I have no schedule for the day |
| ☐ I am highly productive | ☐ I can relax and not feel guilty |
| ☐ I organize something | ☐ I am invited and just have to show up |
| ☐ I can be creative | ☐ I can accomplish something |
| ☐ I am intellectually stimulated | ☐ I do things that don't require me to think too much |
| ☐ I socialize with people | ☐ I am alone or in the company of my spouse |
| ☐ I am athletic | ☐ I do nothing too strenuous |
| ☐ I volunteer/help others | ☐ I can work on my own things |
| ☐ I see/do new things | ☐ I engage in familiar tasks/activities |
| ☐ I travel | ☐ I am at home |
| ☐ I solve problems | ☐ I am not burdened with problems/issues |
| ☐ I have extended time with children/grandchildren | ☐ I can enjoy discrete visits with my children/grandchildren |
| ☐ I win in golf, tennis, or some other sporting event | ☐ I enjoy time with friends playing golf, tennis, or some other sporting event |

## Section 3—The Lowlights

*Create your personal "What Bugs Me" list.*

1. **What have been the lowlights of:**
   a. My past year
   b. My most recent job
   c. My career
   d. My community life
   e. My marriage/partnership

## Section 4—Legacy Matters

1. **Let's say your old college friend is reading an update on graduates prior to attending your 50th college reunion. He is now reading what the reporter wrote about you. Complete your story beginning with the sentence . . .**

   *After leaving a highly successful career at X company, <your name>*

   *_____ . . .*

   *During that time, <your name> also _____ . . .*

   *A close friend of <your name> said _____ about him/her . . .*

   *You will most often find <your name> doing _____ . . .*

2. **What "things" would you most like to impact in your lifetime?**
   a. Are there any "causes" that you feel especially drawn to?
   b. Are there any not-for-profit organizations you would like to become more active with?
   c. Is there anything on your "What Bugs Me" list that you would be excited to tackle/change/fix?

3. **How do you wish your children/grandchildren to remember you? How will they come to know your life stories, experiences, accomplishments?**

## Section 5—Things You Hope to Do Post-Transition

*Check all that apply.*

☐ Have more leisure time

☐ Work out regularly

☐ Travel

☐ Golf/tennis/other sports

☐ Engage in extreme physical adventures

☐ Volunteer (please indicate if you have specific ideas about with whom)

☐ Continue with a corporate career

☐ Start own company

☐ Consult/advise

☐ Take classes, earn degree

☐ Teach

☐ Lecture/speaking opportunities

☐ Mentor/tutor young people

☐ Be outdoors more

☐ Cook (more often)

☐ Entertain friends (more often)

☐ Learn new language

☐ Board service
 ○ Publicly traded company
 ○ Small/mid-size but established
 ○ Startup
 ○ Not-for-profit
 ○ Private Equity/VC

☐ Not-for-Profit
 ○ Board Member
 ○ Management
 ○ Volunteer
 ○ Special Projects

☐ Paint/draw

☐ Garden

☐ Spend (more) time with children/grandchildren

☐ Coach/train

☐ Write

☐ Photography

☐ Master new skill

☐ Work with my hands

☐ Be a caregiver to others

☐ Church/synagogue work

☐ Deepen my faith

☐ Other...

## Section 6—Your Marriage/Partnership

1.  **How would you describe the current state of your marriage partnership?**

    - We operate mostly in parallel and connect occasionally as needed.
    - We operate mostly in parallel, because that's what the job has required of us, but we connect whenever we can and enjoy that time together.
    - We operate well, both independently and together—and look forward to having more together time.
    - We operate mostly as a team and expect that to continue into the future.
    - We operate mostly as a team and look forward to more individual exploration in retirement.
    - Other (please elaborate).

2.  **What would make this the very best season of your marriage/ partnership?**

## Section 7—Spouse/Partner's Input

*(This section is to be completed by your spouse/partner only.)*

1.  **You have been asked to submit (anonymously) responses to the following questions about your spouse/partner:**
    a.  Who is this person at the core?
    b.  What does he/she stand for?
    c.  What makes him/her tick?
    d.  When is he/she the happiest?
    e.  What frustrates him/her?
    f.  Of what is he/she proudest in life? (either personal or work)

2.  **What hopes and concerns do you have about your spouse's/partner's "retirement"?**

3.  **Describe your perfect "day in the life" —post-transition—for you and your spouse/partner.**

## B. Your Next Season Plan: Sample Framework

1. My priorities in this Next Season are
2. What I love
3. Criteria for what I want to do in my Next Season
4. What I am positively *not* interested in doing
5. Some possibilities given my current thinking
6. What I would like to try (first) in the next three to six months

---

*Example: "Joseph's" Next Season Framework*

### Joseph's Priorities

1. Regain health
2. Reconnect with my daughters
3. Do something that is helpful to others (e.g., help build homes or distribute food)
4. Improve my golf game
5. Reconnect with college friends through alumni network

### What Joseph Loves

1. Being with others—I do not enjoy being alone
2. Working with my hands; I love to build things or do physical things while interacting with people
3. Playing golf

### Criteria for What to Do in Next Season

1. Use my dormant skills in woodworking/building things
2. Allow time to exercise, spend time with family, and give back
3. Connect often with other people
4. Enjoy my coffee every morning

### Things Not Interested In

1. Anything that creates stress
2. Working in isolation
3. Anything that precludes my being able to play golf a couple of times per week

### Possibilities

1. Survey local needs for building/construction assistance (e.g., Habitat for Humanity)
2. Find a regular golf group that plays at my level
3. Hire a personal trainer to pull together an exercise routine that works with my schedule and physical condition

---

## C. Working Through Your PARTNER Framework

Below is a framework to guide the conversation with your spouse/partner as you assemble a shared vision and plan for your Next Season. It is helpful to work through the framework independently first, and then discuss it together as you pull together a shared plan.

| | |
|---|---|
| **P**riorities | What are your individual priorities for this Next Season? What are your priorities as a couple? Write your top 10 list, both individually and as a couple. |
| **A**lternatives | You have considered what you might do in this next phase of your life. What are your ideas? How you will spend your time? Where will you live? To what will you dedicate your time and resources? |
| **R**ealities | What current realities/concerns do you have as you enter your Next Season? What realities must you navigate as you make your plans? Are there constraints you must work with, like aging parents or health concerns? Or that you want to work with, like proximity to children or not-for-profits you have committed to? *Note: Do not rush through this phase. It is important to understand one another's concerns entering this phase—and to openly acknowledge variables that enable or constrain your options.* |
| **T**ogetherness | Some things you will want to do together, whereas other activities you will opt to pursue independently. What activities do you hope to share? |
| **N**on-togetherness | Likewise, what do you see yourselves doing independently? *Note: Healthy independence is extremely important in this phase of life. You have each carved independent paths, and you need to honor those desires and commitments as well as adding new ones together.* |
| **E**vents | What actions or next steps do you need to take in light of what you've discussed/agreed to here? |
| **R**evisiting Our Plan | When will you revisit what you've discussed/ agreed to here to see if adjustments need to be made? |

# Your Authors

## Leslie Wilk Braksick, Ph.D.

DR. LESLIE BRAKSICK is the co-founder of MY NEXT SEASON, along with Mark Linsz. Working with Fortune 500 corporations, universities, and government agencies, MY NEXT SEASON is positively impacting the lives of transitioning executives, the organizations they are leaving, and the communities in which they live, by helping executives transition from corporate careers to new life seasons anchored in purpose.

Prior to starting MY NEXT SEASON, Leslie co-founded a management consultancy, CLG (The Continuous Learning Group). Leslie led CLG as its Chairman, President, and CEO, personally consulting to its seniormost clients for 21 years, including GE, Chevron, Heinz, ExxonMobil, The Hartford, Tenet Healthcare, Ingersoll Rand, and many more.

Leslie is a prolific author. Her first book—*Unlock Behavior, Unleash Profits*—was a *Wall Street Journal* Business Best Seller. Another book, *Preparing CEOs for Success: What I Wish I Knew,* has been hailed as a breakthrough that guides first-time CEOs in their transition to their new roles. In it, Leslie presents wisdom and candid quotes from her interviews of more than two dozen CEOs at Johnson & Johnson, Caterpillar, GE, Pepsico, Bank of America, Bechtel, and other peer companies. She also writes monthly for *Smart Business Magazine*.

Leslie has been honored for her community and business leadership, her philanthropy, and her dedicated service to not-for-profits. She is currently on the boards of Princeton Theological Seminary and Children's Hospital of Pittsburgh.

Leslie was recognized as a distinguished alumna from Western Michigan University, where she earned a doctorate in Applied Behavior Analysis and a master's degree in Industrial Psychology. More recently, she earned a master's in Public Health from Johns Hopkins University.

Leslie and husband Matthew, married over 25 years, are the proud parents of Austin and Madeleine. They reside in a suburb of Pittsburgh, PA.

# William R. K. Innes, D.Eng.

BILL INNES was born in Jamaica, where he spent his pre-school years. He earned a degree in Chemical Engineering from Birmingham University in the UK, where he was subsequently honored with a Doctorate in Engineering.

Bill spent most of his career with ExxonMobil and its Canadian affiliate, leading the chemical and petroleum businesses in Canada, Exxon's chemical business in Europe, and serving as CEO of Exxon in Japan.

He retired as President of ExxonMobil Research and Engineering Company, with responsibility for corporate research and the research-engineering-capital project management supporting ExxonMobil's 44 refining and marketing businesses worldwide.

Bill developed ExxonMobil's Operating Integrity Management System, which has become the industry benchmark for ensuring control of hazardous and environmentally sensitive operations. He also led mega-project developments and executions in China, the Middle East, and North America.

Following retirement from ExxonMobil, Bill has served as an Executive Advisor to CEOs and C-suite leaders of 25 corporations in Europe, India, and North America.

He served as a director of Imperial Oil, Esso Sekiyu, Tonen Corporation, Interprovincial Pipelines, and The Continuous Learning Group. He has also served as President of the Canadian Petroleum Products Institute and as a Trustee of the Liberty Science Center.

Bill and Judy, his wife of 50 years, have journeyed together through 16 homes and 3 continents. They now live on Vancouver Island in British Columbia, close to their son Rob and his family, where they enjoy their Next Season and boating in the beauty of the Pacific North West.

# About my❧nextseason

MY NEXT SEASON was co-founded in 2014 by Dr. Leslie Braksick and Mark Linsz, two seasoned executives who envisioned providing a bridge for retiring executives as they transition from corporate careers oriented to productivity, to new seasons anchored in purpose.

Retirement and other corporate transitions are increasingly initiated by companies (rather than individuals), thus often confronting executives with no time for planning and short lead times for their transition. Because these executives single-mindedly work intensely on behalf of their employers until the day they depart, they have little-to-no time for planning the single greatest transition of their adult lives.

Leslie saw this play out with hundreds of executives over her career of more than two decades as an executive advisor to the seniormost leaders of the Fortune 100. Mark observed the same trend while serving nearly three decades as a corporate executive at Bank of America.

Both shared a strong desire to create a company that would address the entire phenomenon of executive retirement, positively impacting the lives of transitioning executives, the companies they retire from, and the communities where they live.

At the company level, MY NEXT SEASON partners with Chief Human Resource Officers to help them customize an approach to transition support. Some companies seek help for large numbers of retiring executives. Others are concerned with smoothing exits that come earlier than the executives anticipated. Still others encounter a business strategy that necessitates transitioning large numbers of people with little notice. MY NEXT SEASON understands and embraces each unique circumstance and works with HR to create fit-for-purpose solutions for the company and individuals.

At the individual level, executives are matched with a personal Advisor who provides 1:1 support using MY NEXT SEASON'S online tools, *Workbook*, and selected readings. The Advisor also draws upon his/her own experience as a previously transitioned executive. Once clarity and a plan are achieved for what's next, executives transition more smoothly and find fulfillment more quickly in their first Next Season.

Additionally, the company experiences huge retention benefits when those who remain see their coworkers so deeply respected and actively cared for, even at the end of their careers.

*For more information: visit mynextseason.com, email us at info@ mynextseason.com, or call 412–802–9196.*

# Acknowledgments

WHAT MAKES THIS BOOK SO POWERFUL is that it provides a voice for the experiences of so many executives with whom we have worked and interviewed.

Special thanks are given to Co-Founder Mark Linsz, whose shared vision for MY NEXT SEASON and support enable all things to happen well.

We thank those who so kindly shared their journeys with us—the highs and the lows of their experiences: Joe Beck, Frank Berardi, Norm Braksick, Patricia Caffrey, Kathy Callahan, Rob Cañizares, Vanessa Castagna, Dr. Jennifer Daley, Richard Downen, Gary Frey, Toby Graham, Tom Graham, Mark Kutner, Mark Linsz, Randal Linville, Ben Markham, Rich McClure, Lori Tomoyasu McGee, Wayne Murphy, John Peppercorn, Jim Reed, Tom Renyi, Bill Robinson, John Ryan, Laura Schulte, Ted Smyth, Mark Stearns, Charlie Strauss, John Thiel, Eli Thomssen, Burnet Tucker, Jim Unruh, Mark Vachon, Helge Wehmeier, Brenda Wensil, Barry Whaling, and Karen Wimbish.

In addition, we thank those who helped us capture those stories and experiences so we could retell them to a greater audience: Austin Braksick, Matthew Huff, Amy Baldwin, and Kathryn Trice.

We are grateful to our MY NEXT SEASON colleagues who contributed content, editing time, and full partnership on this project: Amy Baldwin, Dr. Jennifer Daley, Debbie Dellinger, Sharon Ingles-Fury, John Landry, Rani Lange, Mark Linsz, and Kathryn Trice. Special thanks to Jim Scattaregia and Fred Schroyer, whose gifts always ensure our work is beautiful.

To those whose work with clients helped to ensure the lessons of this book were carried forward to those who most needed to hear them, we also thank the following Advisors: Frank Berardi, Amy Brinkley, Jean Brinkmann, Nancy Bunce, Mary Cahillane, Vanessa Castagna, Dr. Jennifer Daley, Richard Downen, Christine Eosco, Jaime Pluto Gusdorff, Larry Samuelson, Laura Schulte, Mike Sharp, Mark Stearns, Burnet Tucker, Jim Unruh, Brenda Wensil, and Karen Wimbish.

Appreciation is expressed to those who read an early version of the book and offered their endorsement of it and of the MY NEXT SEASON mission: Marcia Avedon, Frank Berardi, Nancy Bunce, Don Campbell, Rob Cañizares, Kathryn A. Cassidy, Vanessa Castagna, David Clair, Neil Cotty, L. Kevin Cox, Hal Cramer, Mike D'Ambrose, Tom DiDonato, Richard Downen, Vicki Escarra, Trevor Fetter, Ed Galante, Marty Gervasi, Lynne Greene, Paul G. Haaga, Jr., Dan Hawkins, Ed Kangas, David Kasiarz, Alan and Carol Kelly, Ken Lewis, W.A. Macdonald, Mindy Mackenzie, Dee Mellor, Susan Peters, Dick Pettingill, Joe Price, Michael Ramage, Lloyd Reeb, Laura Schulte, Mike Sharp, Gary Sheffer, David Simms, Andrea Smith, Julie Smith, Anne Steele, John Thiel, Burnet Tucker, Jim Unruh, Robb Webb, Brenda Wensil, and Patrick Wright.

Finally, we give thanks to the unsung heroes in our lives who, through their unwavering love and support, enable us to do all that we do well: Matt, Austin, and Madeleine; Judy, Rob, Crystal, and Malcolm; and Becky, Ashley, Anna, and Ellie.

Made in the USA
Columbia, SC
25 November 2017